Defensive Softball Drills

Jacquie Joseph, MBA
Michigan State University

Human Kinetics

For my late father, Edward P. Joseph, and my mother, Sally Shaheen Joseph—my first coaches, and the best I could have ever had.

Library of Congress Cataloging-in-Publication Data

Joseph, Jacquie, 1962-
    Defensive softball drills / Jacquie Joseph.
        p.   cm.
    ISBN 0-88011-715-X (pbk.)
    1. Softball--Coaching.   2. Softball--Training.   I. Title.
GV881.4.C6J67   1998
796.357'24--dc21   98-16560
                                                              CIP

ISBN-10: 0-88011-715-X
ISBN-13: 978-0-88011-715-9

Acquisitions Editor: Kenneth Mange; **Developmental Editor:** Julie A. Marx; **Assistant Editor:** Laura Ward Majersky; **Copyeditor:** Amie Bell; **Proofreader:** Erin Cler; **Graphic Designer:** Robert Reuther; **Graphic Artist:** Tara Welsch; **Cover Designer:** Jack Davis; **Cover Photographer:** MSU Sports Information; **Interior Photographers:** Tom Roberts; Kevin W. Fowler/MSU Sports Information (pp. 1, 15, 61, 95, 123); **Illustrator:** Joe Bellis; **Printer:** United Graphics

Human Kinetics books are available at special discounts for bulk purchase. Special editions or book excerpts can also be created to specification. For details, contact the Special Sales Manager at Human Kinetics.

Printed in the United States of America   10   9   8

Human Kinetics
Web site: www.HumanKinetics.com

United States: Human Kinetics
P.O. Box 5076
Champaign, IL 61825-5076
800-747-4457
e-mail: humank@hkusa.com

Canada: Human Kinetics
475 Devonshire Road Unit 100
Windsor, ON N8Y 2L5
800-465-7301 (in Canada only)
e-mail: orders@hkcanada.com

Europe: Human Kinetics
107 Bradford Road
Stanningley, Leeds LS28 6AT
United Kingdom
+44 (0) 113 255 5665
e-mail: hk@hkeurope.com

Australia: Human Kinetics
57A Price Avenue, Lower Mitcham
South Australia 5062
08 8277 1555
e-mail: liaw@hkaustralia.com

New Zealand: Human Kinetics
Division of Sports Distributors NZ Ltd.
P.O. Box 300 226 Albany
North Shore City, Auckland
0064 9 448 1207
e-mail: info@humankinetics.co.nz

Contents

Drill Finder

DRILL #	DRILL	Workable indoors	Small group drills	Partner drills	Conditioning	Many throws	Minimal throws	Page #
1	Three-Quarter Throwing	✓	✓	✓			✓	18
2	Backhand Flips	✓		✓			✓	20
3	Forehand Flips	✓	✓				✓	22
4	Fielding Backhands	✓		✓			✓	24
5	Two-Knees Fielding	✓		✓	—		✓	26
6	Diving	✓		✓			✓	28
7	Fielding Bunts—Corners	✓	✓			✓		30
8	Fielding Squeeze Bunts—Corners	✓	✓				✓	32
9	Angle Back With Cones	✓	✓			✓	✓	34
10	Five-Ball Drill	✓	✓		✓	✓		36
11	Pop-Ups—Infielders		✓				✓	38
12	Live Rundowns	✓	✓				✓	40
13	Four-Corner Infield	✓	✓			✓	✓	42
14	Multiple Infield	✓	✓			✓	✓	44
15	Blind Ball Toss	✓		✓			✓	46
16	Footwork on a Force Out	✓	✓	✓			✓	48
17	Footwork on a Tag Play	✓	✓	✓			✓	50
18	Fielding Bad Throws	✓	✓	✓			✓	52
19	Footwork on a Double Play—Shortstop	✓	✓			✓		54
20	Footwork on a Double Play—Second Baseman	✓	✓			✓		58

(Left margin label spanning the table: **Infielder drills**)

Drills marked both "Many throws" and "Minimal throws" are drills that contain several throws but can be modified easily to remove the throwing element by having fielders toss balls in a bucket or toss them to the side instead. Drills marked as both "Small group drills" and "Partner drills" are explained from a partner perspective but can be modified easily to include larger groups of fielders.

(continued)

v

Acknowledgments

I would like to thank my family, the first team I was on — my older sister, Barbara Rose, who taught me how to compete in our backyard; my brother, John Edward, the funniest and most handsome man I know; my sister, Stephanie Michele, a true example of "walking the walk"; and my sister Allison Ann, a gift of constant joy.

I also thank my assistant, Kim McKeon. She spent many hours helping me recall and record the drills in this book. She has been with me every step. Coaching is a lot more fun with you, Kim, than without you. And thank you to all of my former players for teaching me the most important lessons in coaching and for putting up with me while I learned.

I have had tremendous role models in coaching; if I can make a difference in my players' lives the way these coaches have made a difference in mine, I know I will have accomplished something special. I thank the coaches for whom I have played, including Nancy Clark, Mary Schmidt, Pat O'Berry, Jolynn Vita, Margo Jonker, Pete Menefield, and Danny Woods.

I also thank the coaches I have studied over the years and who have helped me develop: Marcy Weston, Gayle Blevins, Diane Stephenson, Carol Hutchins, Jaci Clark, Kathy Veroni, Rayla Allison, Gloria Becksford, Sharon Backus, Sue Enquist, Mike Candrea, Linda Wells, and Jay Miller.

Finally, I give a very special thank you to Carol E. Anderson for helping me see that all I ever wanted to do was coach.

Introduction

Four recent trends in the game of fastpitch softball—livelier balls; increased bat technology; the left-handed slapper; and, at the collegiate level, the greater distance from the pitching mound to the plate—have all resulted in greater offense (both hits and runs scored). This situation puts tremendous pressure on the defense. To keep pace with these trends in the game, successful coaches and programs must adapt their defensive philosophies.

With this in mind, I share with you the four major defensive philosophies we have developed at Michigan State University:

1. **Eliminate the big inning**—Your opponents will score runs. Giving up only one run should not cost the team the game; however, your team cannot allow the other team to score three or four runs an inning.

2. **Play catch well**—By this we mean make the game simple. We must throw, catch, and field the ball well. Good fielding also includes developing quick feet, a quick release, and soft hands.

3. **Increase the aggressive defensive style with increased player ability**—We expect aggressive play from the more skilled players. But we do not ask players to attempt defensive plays that they are not capable of executing. For example, we would not ask a corner player without a good arm to throw to second on a bunt with a runner on first base.

4. **Work hard on the mental aspect**—We expect errorless defense; but if we do make a mistake, we try to make sure the opponent does not score a run as a result. The team as a whole needs to elevate their level of play rather than letting one player's mistake negatively affect the team's performance. By "elevating our play," we mean that everyone on the team has to step up to cover a teammate's mistake so that we can complete the inning with minimal damage.

Defensive Softball Drills provides practice activities that will help you learn and develop all the skills necessary to become a consistent defensive team. The drill finder will help you identify drills for a variety of practice needs, including drills workable indoors, drills suitable for either partners or small groups, and drills with minimal and many throws. Chapter 1 includes clear descriptions and photographs of the most fundamental softball skills: throwing and catching, fielding ground balls, and catching fly balls. Chapters 2 through 4 focus on specific drills for infielders, pitchers and catchers, and outfielders, respectively. Chapter 5 covers drills that can be utilized by the entire team, and chapter 6 covers my practice recommendations for organizing your workouts to cover all the defensive skills practiced in the drills presented in chapters 2 through 5. You can use the sample practice plans in chapter 6 to help guide you in planning for your own practices.

The 66 drills in *Defensive Softball Drills* provide you with fun, challenging practice activities that cover almost every defensive situation. Regardless of your team's playing level or experience, the drills in this book help you learn and practice the defensive fundamentals necessary for challenging even the best offense. The drills presented here will help your players meet the demands that fastpitch softball places on the defense. Most of these drills, however, can also be used for slow-pitch players. I also have included more and less difficult variations for many of the drills to help you modify them to suit the skill levels of your players.

To ensure you'll be ready to face even the toughest offense, one of your goals as a coach and player should be to hone your defensive skills through practices that simulate gamelike situations as closely as possible—*Defensive Softball Drills* will help you meet that goal.

Key to Diagrams

P = Pitcher

C = Catcher

1B = 1st baseman

2B = 2nd baseman

3B = 3rd baseman

SS = Shortstop

LF = Left fielder

CF = Center fielder

RF = Right fielder

BR = Base runner

CO = Coach

F = Fielder

H = Hitter

R = Receiver

T = Thrower/tosser

= Cones

= Softballs

——————————— = Path of player

—— —— —— = Path of throw

- - - - - - - - - - - - = Path of batted ball

1

Fundamentals

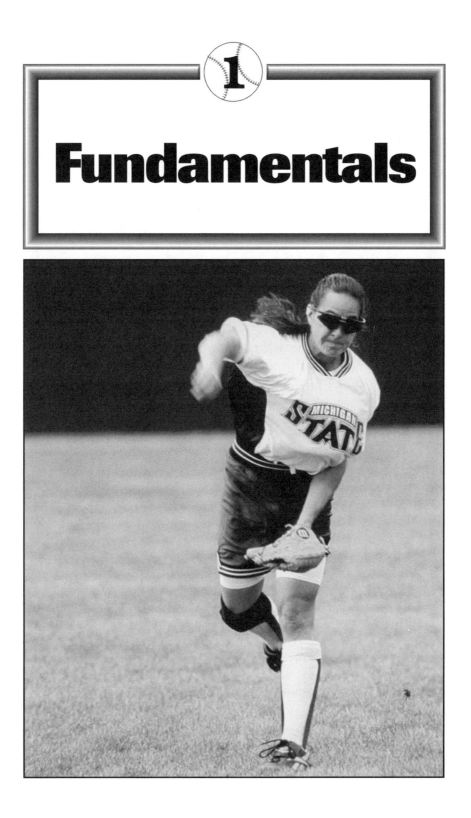

As a coach I assume that each player knows nothing about the basic softball skills at the start of each season. At Michigan State we start over every year and every player with the basic fundamentals of the game. From our All Americans to our incoming freshmen, we stress the basics during our skill development phase with the belief that the team that "plays catch well" usually performs the best defensively.

Remember that *if the team executes in practice they will execute in the game.* A coach cannot expect a team that doesn't catch, throw, or field the ball successfully in practice to somehow figure it out at game time. To help you develop basic defensive skills, this chapter explores the fundamentals of catching, throwing, and fielding.

CATCHING AND THROWING

Work on proper throwing and catching mechanics *every* day in practice. Because almost all throws begin with a catch, I teach my athletes how to receive the ball properly to make the best throw possible. When receiving the ball, it's important for the fielder to move to catch the ball on the throwing side of her body. She should make the catch with both hands to prepare to get rid of the ball quickly. As she receives the ball, she sets her back foot perpendicular to the target (turns sideways to the target) while her front foot points at the target to prepare for the next throw (see figure 1.1). To ensure a proper grip while getting the ball out of the glove quickly, the fielder should press the ball against the glove and into her fingertips.

The first step in learning how to throw properly is understanding four-seam rotation throwing. Regardless of a player's position, mastering proper throwing mechanics is critical, not only for the player's future athletic potential but also to reduce the chance of an injury to her throwing arm. To begin, instruct the players to hold the ball so the two horizontal long seams are visible; they should then grip the ball on these seams using the pads of their fingertips (see figure 1.2). The middle finger should be placed in the middle of the ball on the seam, and the thumb should be placed directly opposite the middle finger on the opposite seam. The index finger and the ring finger are placed on either side of the middle finger on the seam as well. Instruct players to allow the pinky finger to relax on the side

Figure 1.1   Foot placement when receiving the throw.

of the ball. They should grip the ball using the pads of the fingertips—it shouldn't be pushed deep into the hand. A tool in helping players see the four-seam rotation when throwing is to draw a half inch line across the four seams with a black felt marker. When the player throws the ball she should see a straight vertical line.

If the player's hand is too small to place her fingers and thumb on a seam, have her lay her thumb on the slick part of the ball, keeping it directly opposite her middle finger. You may find it helpful to use an 11-inch ball while teaching, especially with younger athletes. Players with very large hands and long fingers may be able to grip the ball with two fingers. In this case, the thumb should be placed directly opposite the midpoint of the middle and index fingers.

Once players understand four-seam throwing, they can grab the ball in any fashion during practice as long as they get at least some fingers on any seam. Understanding four-seam

Figure 1.2　Four-seam rotation grip.

throwing becomes more important during wet conditions when the ball is slippery.

The athlete begins the throwing motion by moving the throwing hand down along her throwing side past the upper thigh while pointing the glove hand toward the target. She then brings the throwing arm up behind the body and points the ball in the direction opposite the throw (figure 1.3). The forward motion begins by simultaneously bringing the throwing arm forward, leading with a high elbow and keeping the hand behind the ball, and bringing the glove hand back toward the torso, curling the glove to the body (figure 1.4). The player then releases the ball toward the intended target (figure 1.5) and follows through with a relaxed arm to the opposite hip.

FIELDING

All infielders and outfielders should assume the basic ready position before each pitch. In the basic ready fielding position, the player should stand on the balls of her feet with her knees bent, her legs slightly wider than shoulder-width apart, and

Figure 1.3 Bring the throwing arm up behind the body and point the ball in the direction opposite the throw.

Figure 1.4 Begin the forward motion by simultaneously bringing the throwing arm forward, keeping the hand behind the ball, and bringing the glove hand back toward the torso.

Figure 1.5   Release the ball toward the intended target and follow through with a relaxed arm to the opposite hip.

her feet slightly toed in. Her arms hang out in front of the body around knee height, with the palm of the glove and hand facing out toward the ball. The position of the arms varies slightly depending on the defensive position:

* Corners should place the glove low and almost touching the ground (figure 1.6).
* Middle infielders should hang the glove and throwing hand at knee height (figure 1.7).
* Outfielders should hang the glove and throwing hand at the waist (figure 1.8).

Ground Balls

The fundamentals of fielding a ground ball are the same regardless of the defensive position. All fielders should attack the ball rather than letting the ball "play them." The athlete must reach out for the ball with her glove flat on the ground and

Figure 1.6   Corner ready position.

Figure 1.7   Middle infield ready position.

Figure 1.8   Outfield ready position.

the palm up, then transfer the ball from the glove to the throwing hand as quickly as possible while ensuring a proper grip.

Infielders

As the ball approaches, the fielder should reach out to field the ball (figure 1.9a). As the ball is fielded the glove should be flat on the ground (glove hand palm up, not fingers pointing down to the ground), and the throwing hand should turn so that the palm is facing down and is placed on top of the ball when it enters the glove (figure 1.9b). Using soft hands (see **drill #5, Two-Knees Fielding**) the infielder "gives" with the ball, bending her elbows and bringing the glove and ball toward her stomach, keeping her head down. The glove is used to transfer the ball from the field into the throwing hand.

Outfielders

Outfielders use three primary methods to field balls hit on the ground; the decision of which fielding method to use depends on the game situation, the field conditions, and the outfielder's abilities.

a

b

Figure 1.9 (a) The infielder should reach out for the ball with the glove flat on the ground, then (b) turn the throwing hand so that the palm is placed on top of the ball when it enters the glove.

1. **Down and block**—This method is the most conservative and most frequently used method. The outfielder first positions herself to field the ball in the center of her body. As she begins to field the ball, she rotates the right knee (for right-handed throwers) down to the ground so the lower leg is perpendicular to the line from which the ball came, forming an "L" shape. The shoulders should be rounded and square to the ball, with the chin tucked down. As the ball approaches the glove, the outfielder reaches out with the glove (keeping it flat with the pocket facing up) and places the opposite hand on top of the ball as it enters the glove, just like fielding any other ball. When the player develops enough leg strength, the knee can come close to, but not actually touch, the ground (figure 1.10). Use this fielding technique for routine grounders when it won't be necessary to throw a runner out, and when field conditions are poor.

2. **Like an infielder**—When the ball is hit on the ground to the outfield and a potential play is at a base, the outfielder should field the ball like an infielder. The fielder begins by moving or charging to field the ball in the center of the body

Figure 1.10   Down and block.

(figure 1.11a). As she begins to field the ball, she bends her knees and leans slightly forward at the waist. The fielder should reach out for the ball, with the glove flat (pocket facing up), and place the opposite hand on top of the ball to lock the ball in (like an infielder), making sure to use soft hands ("give" with the ball) as she catches the ball (figure 1.11b).

Figure 1.11 Like an infielder: *(a)* Field the ball in the center of the body, *(b)* using soft hands to bring the ball in.

3. **On the charge**—This technique should be used only when an outfielder is attempting to throw out a runner in a critical game situation. When the ground ball is hit, the outfielder charges the ball so that she will field the ball as close to her left foot as possible (for right-handed throwers) without tripping herself. The head goes down as the glove goes down to field, and the glove touches the ground as the player scoops the ball off the ground (figure 1.12). The fielder should run through the ball as she fields it, then come up, set her feet, and throw the ball all in one motion. Momentum should carry the player forward, and she should end up in front of where the ball was fielded. Charging the ball should not be attempted if the outfield is in poor condition.

Fly Balls

Every player on the field must learn how to field fly balls. Infielders have to be able to catch routine infield fly balls as well as go back and judge "tweeners" into the outfield. Out-

Figure 1.12 On the charge.

fielders need to catch balls hit all around them, and pitchers and catchers need to practice catching pop-ups. Ideally, all balls should be caught chest high on the throwing side with the body set to throw toward the target before the ball is caught (figure 1.13).

Balls hit over a player's head are the most difficult to handle, and each player should be taught to "drop step turn and run." To teach this skill we do what we call the **Quarterback Catch drill (#52)**. The player first decides to what side of her body the ball has been hit, next she drop steps with the foot on the same side of the ball, and last she turns her entire body and runs for the ball. For example, if the ball is hit to the player's right, the player should drop step with the right foot first. It is important that as the player runs she keeps the ball on *one side* of her body; she should not run directly underneath the ball. This sideways alignment helps the fielder track the ball as it moves

Figure 1.13   Catch fly balls at chest height on the throwing side.

through the air. When drop stepping, the player should look back for the ball with her head only. Instruct players to avoid backpedaling at all costs.

Every successful defensive play depends on each player executing these fundamental catching, throwing, and fielding skills consistently under game pressure. The next four chapters present drills for specific positions and for the whole team to work on the basic fundamentals presented here.

Infielder Drills

C hoosing which players are suited for which infield positions can be a difficult task. During the try-out phase I like to begin with **Line Fielding (drill #57)**. In observing the team execute this drill, the coach can get a read on players' ranges and who handles the glove well from what distances. Have each infielder field balls at both corner and middle infield depth. After 5-10 minutes, line them all up at either third base or shortstop. Fungo from home plate and have each player field 10 balls in both positions; next, switch all players to either first or second base and repeat fielding 10 balls at both spots. Some players are natural right-side players, whereas others seem more suited for the left side. The line fielding drill allows the coach to determine which players tend to "see" the ball better from the left side and which tend to "see" the ball better from the right side.

Middle infielders should be able to handle more of a throwing range than corner players, whereas corner players must be able to handle the glove quickly for handling or catching line shots and playing very close to the batter. The first baseman must have good hands because she will be involved in almost every play. Because the throws are longer from shortstop, this player usually has a stronger arm than the second baseman.

Left-handed players pose a special situation. Typically, if left-handers want to play infield, not including pitching and catching, they should play first base. Lefties are more suited to play first base, any outfield position, and pitcher, but factor in players' desires and overall athleticism when delegating positions. Although there is no question that ideals regarding positions and body types exist, just remember that coaches are dealing with *people*. I was on a state championship caliber team with a left-handed second baseman who went on to play at a competitive Division III university.

Positionally, the first and third basemen play in front of the bases as far back as they can while still being able to field a surprise bunt. This usually ends up placing them approximately 35-50 feet away from the batter depending on the players' skill levels. The infielders should move in and back depending on the game situation and the batters' tendencies. For example, with a runner on first and no outs, the corners need to play in to cover the expected bunt. The shortstop should play as far back as possible to maximize the ground she can cover while still being able to field a routine ground ball and get the player out at first. Lesser skilled players should position themselves nearer the baseline. The same adjustments need to be made for shortstop depending on the game situation and the batters' tendencies. For example, with a runner on first and less than two outs, the shortstop should play at a depth where she can get to second if the runner attempts to steal second. The quicker the shortstop, the deeper she can play.

When choosing the infield, coaches of younger, less skilled athletes should take into consideration that on youth teams infielders tend to field more balls than do outfielders. Coaches should begin by placing their best athletes on the mound, behind the plate, and at shortstop and then build the rest of the infield from there.

The most common errors on the infield involve the basic fundamentals of throwing and catching. Games are most often won and lost not on complex first and third situations and pickoffs, but on the basic fundamentals. Throwing errors occur most often because of a poor grip, a bad exchange when transferring the ball from the glove into the throwing hand, or rushing the throw before the ball is securely positioned in the fingers of the throwing hand. Ideally, players want to move toward the ball as quickly as possible while remaining in control of their movements. To begin, slow the players down and concentrate on basic fielding and throwing mechanics. By taking time to first set the body properly, the player will more than make up for that "lost" time with a strong, accurate throw. The player whose feet are set properly will now potentially only miss the target high and low. They have eliminated the potential for missing the target to the left and right.

Other errors occur when players compound errors during one play. Teach players to throw the ball only when they have an excellent chance of getting an out; many times the smart play may be to hold the ball after an error to minimize the damage. A player who has made one mistake may have cost the team one run, but compounding mistakes could cost the team many runs in the same inning.

The drills in this chapter cover almost every possible infield situation, from routine grounders, fly balls, and footwork at the bases to special situations like fielding bunts and handling rundowns. Adjust each to the skill levels of your players to cover all of the essential infielder skills listed in chapter 6.

Three-Quarter Throwing

Purpose: To teach the sidearm throw, used primarily by the middle infielders for short distance throws of about 10-15 feet.

Procedure

1. Two players stand approximately 5-8 feet apart, facing opposite directions but on the same plane (like on a foul line). Both players are in the ready fielding position.

2. One player, in a corner ready position (ready position for first and third basemen, see chapter 1), drops the ball in front of her. She picks the ball up with both hands and releases it with a sidearm motion to her partner. The standing partner receives the ball at chest height.

3. After receiving the ball, the player gets into the corner ready position and repeats the sidearm throw back to her partner.

4. Increase the distance between players as control is gained.

5. Each player makes 10 sidearm throws successfully.

Variations

- Allow players having difficulty with this skill to use a modified throw in which the feet still stay planted but the throw is the conventional "over the top" throw with a shorter arm swing to aid in getting rid of the ball quickly.

- Place all infielders in a line, facing alternating directions. Starting at one end of the line, have players throw sidearm from one to the next all the way to the end of the line. Then have each player face the opposite direction and throw back down the line.

Backhand Flips

Purpose: To teach the flip used as a throw when players are within close range of the target and on the backhand side. Using this technique ensures that the ball will not be over-thrown.

Procedure

1. Position partners as in **drill #1, Three-Quarter Throwing**.

2. The players are in corner ready position. Player one drops the ball straight down, close to the middle of her body. With knees bent and chest parallel to the ground, she scoops up the ball with both hands and places it in her throwing hand. She then lifts her elbow so that the tricep is parallel with her back and the arm forms a 90-degree angle at the elbow. She extends her hand toward her partner, flipping the ball in her partner's direction at waist height. The partner in turn drops the ball and flips it back.

3. Players should flip the ball to each other 15-30 times or until the skill is mastered.

Key Point

- Upon release the hand should not rise above the height of the shoulder. Players should not flip the wrist, causing the fingers to point upward.

Variation

- Combine **drills #2, Backhand Flips** and **#3, Forehand Flips**, using the setup in **drill #2**. One player practices the backhand flip to a partner and the partner forehand flips it back, then players switch skills.

3 Forehand Flips

Purpose: To teach the flip used as a throw when players are within close range of the target from the forehand side. Using this technique can cut down on overthrows. The forehand flip is primarily used by the shortstop when shoveling the ball to second base when within short range of second but not close enough (farther than 5 feet away) to take the bag herself, and by the second baseman when shoveling the ball to first after fielding the ball in the gap.

Procedure

1. Begin by placing infielders in a line at the shortstop position with a receiver at second base.

2. Hit or roll the ball to each player. The player fields the ball then turns her body so her feet are pointing toward second base and her shoulders are square to the target. She then shovels the ball to second base aiming chest high over the base.

3. Hit 10-15 balls to each player or continue until the skill is mastered.

Key Points

- The fielder should stay low with her back at a 45-degree angle to the ground instead of standing up to shovel the ball.

- After shoveling the ball, players should allow their momentum to continue forward toward the target for one or two steps. Players who try to stop and then shovel the ball tend to flip the ball too high.

Fielding Backhands

Purpose: To develop proper fielding technique to field balls hit to the backhand side.

Procedure

1. Partners start in a ready position for corners or middle infielders as described in chapter 1.

2. A partner (or a coach) rolls a ball to the player's backhand side within 3 feet of her body. The fielder rotates toward the ball without picking up her feet (the toes turn and face the direction of the rolling ball), stays low while she takes a crossover step, and turns the glove over and around so the funny bone of her elbow is facing the direction from which the ball came and the glove is open to the ball as she fields it. After fielding the ball the fielder brings her glove hand up to meet her throwing hand to transfer the ball from the glove to the hand quickly.

3. Field 10-15 balls successfully or continue until the skill is mastered, then switch players.

Key Points

- The glove should be held close to the foot (not out away from the body), dragging slightly on the ground, with the fingers pointing down (unlike basic fielding).

- Make sure the player lets the ball come to her rather than reaching too far forward for it.

5 Two-Knees Fielding

Purpose: To develop "soft hands" when fielding a ground ball.

Procedure

1. Partners kneel facing each other about 5 feet apart.

2. One player begins with her arms and glove reaching out in front of her. The glove should be laying flat on the ground with the pocket up not the fingers down.

3. One partner rolls a ball to the other. The fielding partner keeps her glove flat, reaches out, then gives with the ball as it approaches. The elbows come back toward her body (but not into it), moving back along the side of the body while bringing the ball toward the stomach. The fielder must keep her head down and look the ball in.

4. Each partner fields 10-20 balls.

Key Points

- The fielding player must keep her head down and look at the ball as she pulls it in.

- Players can pretend the ball is an egg and "give" (soften in the hands) when receiving it so it doesn't break.

Variations

- Using the same setup, partners throw short one hoppers. Make sure to skip the ball low.

- Use softie balls for younger players.

6 Diving

Purpose: To develop proper technique when diving for ground balls.

Procedure

1. Partners face each other, standing about 15 feet apart.
2. The diving player turns on the balls of the feet, keeping the feet in the same spot, and faces the direction in which she will dive first. The ball should be rolled or tossed in a line drive to the side the player is facing, just out of the reach of the diving fielder.
3. From a semicrouch position, staying low to the ground, the fielder dives out toward the toss. She lands in the dive on her chest and stomach, her body fully extended, her back slightly arched, and her head up.
4. Using this format, practice diving to the left and right. Dive five times in each direction before switching.

Key Points

- When diving out for a ball to the player's non-glove side, the pocket of the glove should face the infield at all times with the thumb down. When diving toward the glove side the pocket of the glove should face the infield with the thumb up.
- Players should catch the ball at its lowest point. Catching the ball too high and then falling could result in the ball becoming dislodged from the glove.

Variations

- For beginners who may be afraid to dive, use a water slide or a large piece of cardboard or wet the grass first.
- The diver takes a few running steps before diving rather than diving from a standstill.
- Practice diving forward for line drives landing in front of the player. When diving forward, the player should land on her forearm, curling the hand up after catching the ball to prevent the web of the glove from hitting the ground and knocking the ball out.

Fielding Bunts—Corners

Purpose: To practice covering the routine bunt situation with a runner on first, less than two outs, and a nonslapper up at the plate.

Procedure

1. The coach is in the batter's box, with receivers at first and second. The first and third basemen play at bunt situation depth (about 25-35 feet from the batter, but adjust for skill level). The coach must compare the batter's skill to each fielder's—the closer the fielder plays the greater the potential for danger if the batter swings away.

2. When the coach indicates a bunt, the first and third basemen should move in as quickly as possible while maintaining control (called *crashing*). Simultaneously, both corners move in 3-4 feet toward the pitcher (called *squeezing*). Moving in toward the pitcher cuts down the gap between the batter and the basemen and puts the fielders in better positions to make throws.

3. The coach then tosses a bunt in front of the plate. The fielder who calls it should surround the ball, fielding the ball on her back foot and aligning her body to throw quickly and get the out at first base.

4. Repeat until all corner players field 10-15 bunts.

Key Points

- Footwork is critical to fielding bunts successfully, and the fielder must set her feet to the base toward which she is throwing. In high school softball, the fielder usually goes for the out at first base. Therefore, the fielder sets her feet as if she is throwing to first. Then if the play is called to go to second, she must reset her feet to throw to second. In college softball, many teams approach the ball as if the throw will go to second base. If the play is called to go to first, players will shift their feet to get the out at first.

- If the first baseman is left handed, she should not squeeze the infield as hard because throws to second base are easier for the lefty.

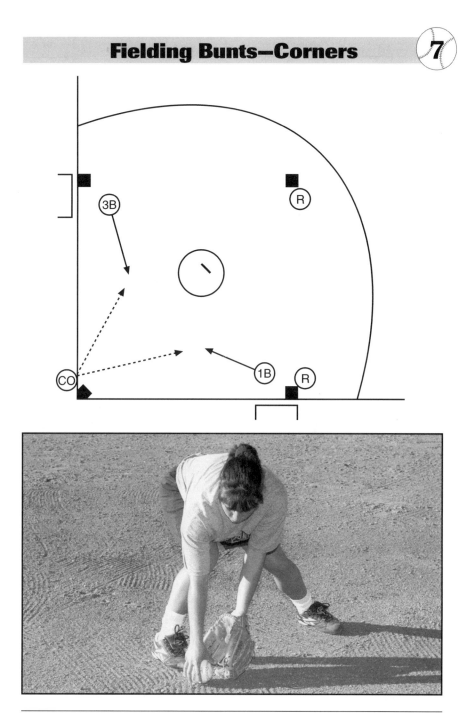

Surround the ball first, aligning the body in the direction of the throw, and pick up the ball on the back foot.

8 Fielding Squeeze Bunts—Corners

Purpose: To practice repetitions in fielding squeeze bunts with a runner on third.

Procedure

1. Both corners are involved in this drill. To begin, the coach squares to bunt. When the fielders recognize the surprise bunt they should crash in the same manner described in **drill #7, Fielding Bunts—Corners**, while maintaining control.

2. The defense yells "Four!" to simulate alerting the infield that the runner on third is breaking to the plate. In a game situation anyone who sees the runner breaking for home can yell "Four!"

3. The fielder who calls the ball surrounds it before fielding it so the ball is on the fielding hand side and in front of the player. She then shovels the ball to the catcher at knee height and slightly up the line.

4. Repeat until all corner players have an opportunity to practice fielding five bunts each.

Key Points

- The defense should watch for a potential squeeze bunt by the offense whenever a quick runner is on third base and there are less than two outs.

- The fielder should stay low and run through the ball, allowing momentum to carry her a step after letting go of the ball. Staying low helps to keep the toss to the plate down.

- The player fields the ball with her bare hand and uses her hand and the back of the glove to shovel the ball to the pitcher, rather than allowing the ball to go into the glove.

Variation

- Use an actual runner at third to create a more gamelike practice.

Angle Back With Cones

Purpose: To improve the middle infielder's footwork when fielding balls hit up the middle or in the hole.

Procedure

1. Set up cones to the right and left of the fielder. Place the cones approximately three steps behind and four steps to the side of the fielder. One tosser (or coach) per two players works best.

2. The fielder begins in ready position facing the tosser, who rolls ground balls to the outside of the cones.

3. The fielder must take a drop step back with the foot on the ball side and then turn and sprint around the cone to the spot. The objective is to cut the ball off and not allow it to get through the infield. By taking an angle the player allows the ball to travel farther, thus giving herself more time to get to it. The fielder can throw the ball back to the tosser or put it in a bucket.

4. Switch fielders on each ball, and have each player field 10-15 balls.

Key Point

• Allow for the player to get around the cone and field the ball in the middle of her body instead of using backhand or forehand fielding techniques to field balls.

Variation

• Once the players improve, hit the balls from home plate.

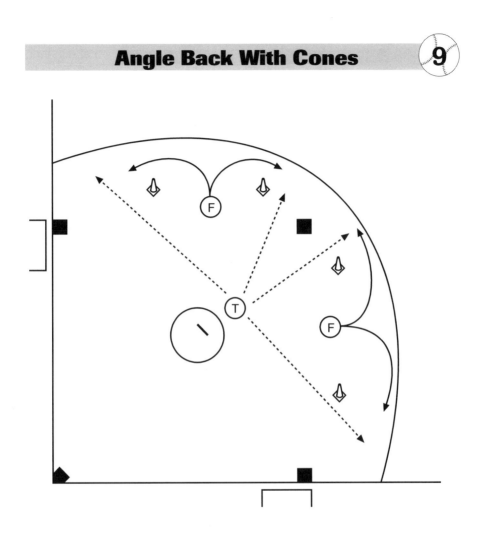

Five-Ball Drill

Purpose: To practice footwork and releasing the ball quickly for the throw. An intense conditioning element is also a part of this drill.

Procedure

1. This drill can be used with any of the infielders in a variety of situations. For each position, place five balls in a line in an area where that player would likely field balls. For example, to help the third baseman practice fielding bunts, set up five balls in a line extending from the foul line toward the pitcher's mound approximately 10 feet away from home plate, where the fielder would pick them up for a bunt.

2. The third baseman starts in her normal ready position and depth, then runs to surround the first ball and throws it to first. She then runs back to her starting position and quickly turns back to field the next ball. Repeat until the fielder throws all five balls.

3. Place the balls in similar areas for the first baseman and catcher. For middle infielders, place the balls to one side of each player and have them practice their throws to each of the bases.

4. Each player fields and throws two sets of five balls placed in slightly different locations.

Variation

- Two fielders can be fielding and throwing at the same time. For example, the first baseman can practice fielding bunts and throwing to first while the third baseman fields bunts and throws to second. Or the first and third basemen can work together to field balls and practice throws while the shortstop and second baseman do the same.

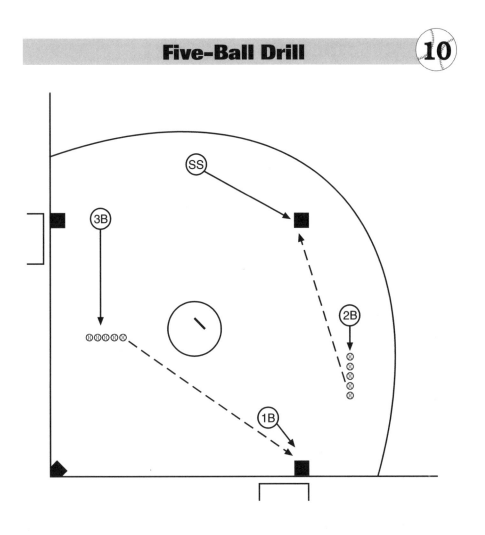

Pop-Ups—Infielders

Purpose: To establish appropriate guidelines for fielders when pop-ups are hit in the infield.

Procedure

1. Place players in their infield positions and hit pop-ups in all areas.
2. The key is to communicate—someone must call the ball each time. Players should only call the ball by saying, "Mine, mine!" Once a player calls for the ball she must catch it, unless there is time for another player to call her off. If a player wants the ball that was already called, she must say, "No, no, mine, mine!"
3. Hit 2-3 pop-ups per position.

Key Points

Fly-ball priorities for infielders are listed next:
- The corners should catch anything hit in front of the base, whether fair or foul.
- The middle infielders should catch anything hit behind the base and fair. If the ball is hit just behind a base and is foul, the corner may have it.
- The pitcher should not catch anything outside of the circle.
- The catcher will handle anything hit directly behind the plate. If the ball is hit just in front of the plate area the catcher or corner can catch it.
- It really does not matter what term the team uses for calling the ball; they should just be consistent and loud.

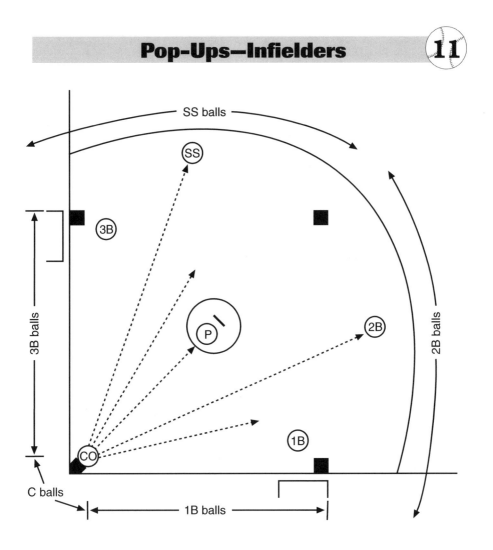

Live Rundowns

Purpose: To execute the rundown successfully.

Procedure

1. Place players at their positions in the infield, including the catcher and pitcher. A coach stands in the middle of the infield with a ball, and base runners are placed halfway between home and first and first and second.

2. The runners begin running the bases, and the coach throws the ball to any player in the infield. The runners continue running so they are caught between two bases, setting up a rundown. The rundown begins on the runner closest to home, and the defensive players fill in where appropriate.

3. A rundown can be executed using one or two throws.

Key Points

- The defensive player first gets the ball up, holding it up with her elbow bent at a 90-degree angle.

- The player waiting to receive the ball should slowly step toward the runner to shorten the base path. Make sure both the thrower and receiver have created a throwing lane by standing on the same side of the base path. They should not throw across the runner.

- With the ball held in the air, the thrower sprints at the runner, running her back to the lower-numbered base. For example, if the player defending first base has the ball, she must first throw it to second base to get the runner running back toward first base.

- When executing a rundown, players must use a *dart throw* to get the ball to their teammates. In executing a dart throw, the player should use only her elbow and wrist to throw the ball by extending the elbow forward as if she were throwing a dart. The throws should all be chest high. The player follows her throw to the next base and stands ready to rotate in to cover the next base in case the rundown continues.

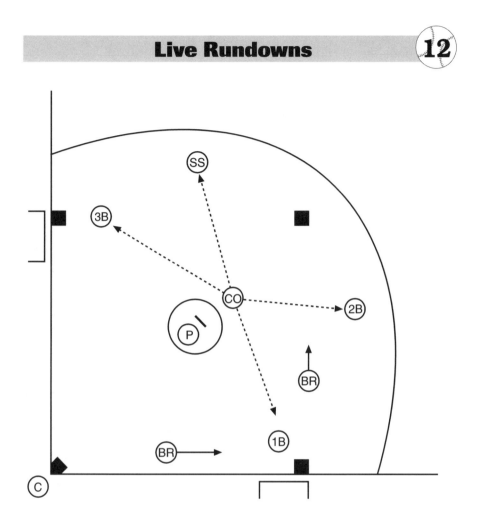

Four-Corner Infield

Purpose: To maximize the number of repetitions of ground balls and to improve skill in fielding ground balls.

Procedure

1. Two sets of partners set up near home plate in foul territory. One set stands on the third base side of home, and the other set stands on the first base side of home, facing the infield. Two additional sets of partners also stand on each foul line closer to the actual bases in foul territory. One partner is going to fungo, and the other partner will receive balls. Two or three infielders go to each position on the infield.

2. Begin hitting balls. Each fielder takes two and rotates to the back of the line. The partners closest to third base hit to the second baseman, the partners closest to home on the third base side hit to the first baseman, the partners on the first base side closest to home hit to the third baseman, and the partners closest to first base on the first base foul line hit to the shortstop.

3. Perform this drill for 10-15 minutes.

Key Point

- To make sure that no one gets hit by a ball, it is important that the hitters stay behind the foul lines and the fielders don't come up too much to charge balls.

Variations

- To improve safety, instead of throwing across the field to the receivers standing with each fungo hitter, the fielders can put the balls in a bucket. This also cuts down on the number of players needed for the drill.
- Vary the difficulty of balls being hit, but be careful not to cross players into each other's territories.

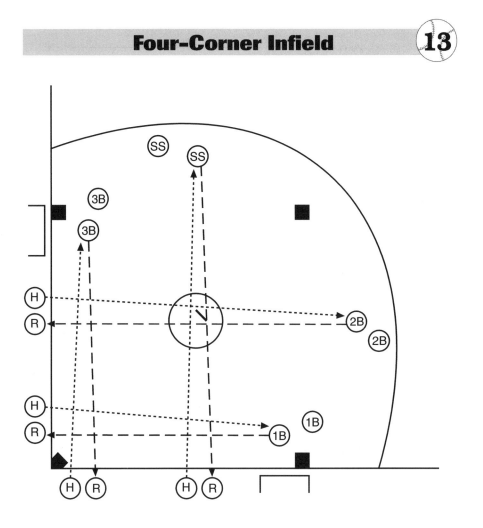

Multiple Infield

Purpose: To create pressure on the defense, to maximize the number of players involved at once, and to practice fielding primarily ground balls and bunts.

Procedure

1. Set up as in **drill #13, Four-Corner Infield**. The person on the third base foul line near third hits to the second baseman, the person on the third base foul line near home hits to the first baseman, the person on the first base foul line near home hits to the third baseman, and the person on the first base foul line near first hits to the shortstop.

2. There are three sets of situations for this drill. The balls can be hit at the same time.

   • Set 1—The players hitting to shortstop and first base are out of the first set. The third baseman fields the ball and throws across to first for a force out with the first baseman covering. The second baseman fields the ball and throws to second base with the shortstop covering.

   • Set 2—The players hitting to second base and third base are out of the second set. The first baseman fields the ball and throws to third while the shortstop fields the ball and throws to second base for force outs.

   • Set 3—The players hitting to shortstop and first base are out of the third set. The third baseman fields a bunt and throws to second base for a force out with the shortstop covering the base while the second baseman fields the ball and throws to first.

3. Do each set for 3-5 minutes or until all players have rotated through or gotten adequate repetitions.

Key Point

   • Follow the guidelines for **drill #13, Four-Corner Infield**, and be sure to think through the situation—safety is the first consideration. With careful planning you can create almost all game situations safely.

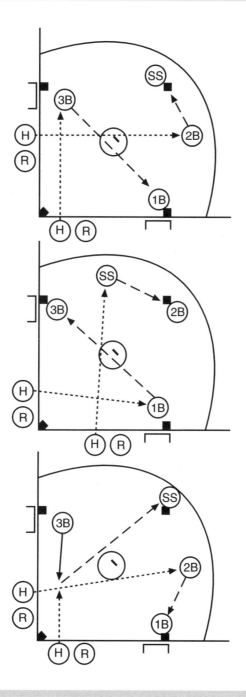

15 Blind Ball Toss

Purpose: To improve reaction time and glove handling.

Procedure

1. This drill needs to be done inside unless a wall is available outside. (Cement or solid wood is ideal. Chain link fencing is not good.) One player sets up in fielding position facing the wall, 5-10 feet away. Her partner is behind the fielder (within 2 feet) with a ball.

2. The tosser throws a ball against the wall in front of the fielder, and the fielder must react and field the ball.

3. Field 10 balls and switch. Repeat two to three times.

Key Points

- The fielder must keep her glove low and her knees bent.
- Fielders should use backhands as needed and shuffle the feet when possible.
- As players improve they should position themselves closer to the wall, and the tosser should throw the ball harder and vary the direction of the throws more often.

Footwork on a Force Out

Purpose: To develop proper footwork at all bases on a force out.

Procedure

1. One player at a time is up at the base, and the coach or a partner throws the fielder balls from different areas of the field. The infielders can also be spread out to their respective bases with multiple throwers.

2. The fielder begins by standing in front of the base with her feet far enough apart to straddle it, toes facing the direction from which the ball is coming. She should stand on the balls of her feet and keep her feet parallel to each other to keep her body squared to the thrower.

3. As the tosser throws the ball, the fielder kicks back her right foot (for a right-hander) and places it on the front edge of the base while she stretches her left leg out and reaches with both hands to receive the ball.

4. Each player catches 7-10 balls.

Key Points

- Make sure the player doesn't prematurely stretch toward the ball before it is thrown.

- An advanced skill is to teach the player to switch which foot is on the base to accommodate an errant throw. For instance, if the throw is to the back side (outfield side) of first base, the first baseman should switch feet, placing her left foot on the base, and stretch toward the ball. In all cases, the players should leave the base if necessary to block errant throws.

Variations

- For beginners or less skilled players, start with the right foot already on the base and then stretch out to the ball.

- One fielder at a time begins in a starting position at one of the bases. When the coach says, "Go," the player turns facing the infield and runs back to the base, then sets up and looks for the throw.

Footwork on a Tag Play

Purpose: To develop proper technique for a tag play at a base. The footwork on a tag play is the same for any base.

Procedure

1. As in **drill #16, Footwork on a Force Out**, players can be up one at a time at one base or at each of their respective bases with multiple throwers. The coach or partner stands near the pitching mound.

2. The coach or partner throws the ball at knee height (as with any tag play) to the bag. The fielder should position herself in front of the bag (facing the incoming runner), taking half of the bag away from the offensive player.

3. After the player receives the ball, she tags the imaginary runner (the back side of the glove is down with the fingers pointing up) and immediately moves toward the infield.

4. Each fielder takes 10-15 throws.

Key Points

• Guard against letting the offensive player tie the defensive player up with a slide. Teach players to make the tag at the base by allowing the runner to slide into the tag instead of reaching out after the runner. Remember, the runner must come to the base to be safe.

• The half of the base the player takes must be on the same side of the bag as the ball. For instance, if the play is at third and the ball is coming from inside the base path (as in a throw from first base), the third baseman must be positioned on the inside of the bag. If the throw is coming from outside the base path (as in a throw from left field) she should position herself on the outside half of the base.

Fielding Bad Throws

Purpose: To develop skills to catch bad throws at any base.

Procedure

1. A tosser sets up with a bucket of balls 10-15 feet away from a player at the base, and the fielder positions herself at the base with her body and feet facing the tosser, as if she was ready to make a force out. This drill can also be practiced with infielders at their respective bases with multiple throwing partners.

2. The tosser throws balls that either hit the dirt or are wide to one side of the bag. As the ball is thrown, the fielder shuffles her feet to catch the ball in the center of her body.

3. Rotate players through 10 times each, allowing them to successfully field 8-10 bad throws.

Key Points

- If the ball is wide but not in the dirt, the fielder should shuffle to the proper side and then kick back to get to the base. For example, instead of kicking back with her right foot (for right-handers), the player can switch feet and kick back with the left foot to field a ball thrown severely to the right.

- If the ball is thrown in the dirt, the fielder should kick back with her right foot; step out with her left leg; bend her knees, touching the ground if necessary; reach out with her glove hand, keeping the glove flat with the pocket facing up (as when fielding a ground ball); and scoop the ball as she would a grounder. She should give with the ball, bending her elbows back toward her body with soft hands (see **drill #5, Two-Knees Fielding**). As soon as possible, the player should place her throwing hand on top of the ball.

- If necessary, the player must leave the base to get the ball to stop an errant throw. Players must not allow the ball to get past the base.

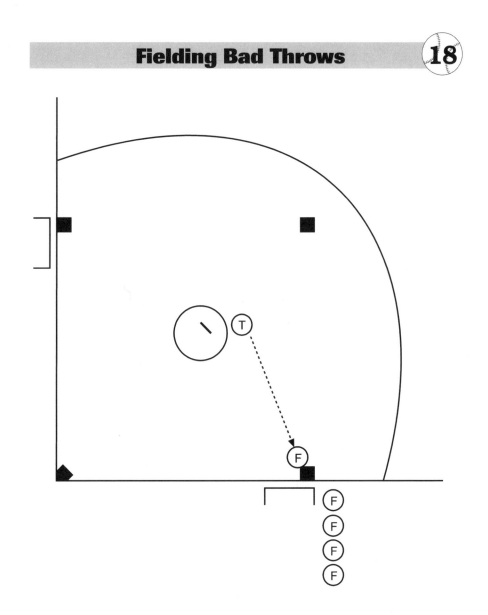

19. Footwork on a Double Play— Shortstop

Purpose: To establish good footwork to turn a double play.

Procedure

1. The fielders line up at the shortstop position and run over to second base one at a time with both hands extended, asking for the ball. (Each fielder yells, "Two, two, two!")

2. The coach (or another tosser) is positioned about halfway between the pitching mound and second base with a bucket of balls, and tosses each fielder a ball as the fielder approaches the base.

3. There are three ways that we use most often for the shortstop to turn the double play.

   - Technique 1—When the thrown ball is coming from within the base path, the shortstop places her left foot on the infield side of second base and in front of the base, pointed toward first *(a)*. She then sweeps the front edge of the bag with her right foot, plants with her right foot, and releases the ball to first *(b)*.

   - Technique 2—When the thrown ball is coming from outside the base path, the shortstop steps across the base toward the ball with her left foot *(a)*. She sweeps the back corner of the bag with her right foot *(b)*, plants with her right foot, and releases the ball to first *(c)*.

   - Technique 3—The easiest method (good for younger players) is for the shortstop to place her left foot on the third base side of second base while also keeping her body on the third base side, receive the ball, step off the bag, set her feet, and throw to first.

4. Each fielder makes 5-10 plays.

Key Point

- The players must receive the ball with both hands up asking for the ball. No matter what, be sure to get the out at second base before throwing to first.

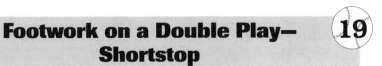

Technique 1
(a) Place left foot in front of the bag, pointing toward first base.

Technique 1
(b) Kick back with the right foot swiping the front edge of the bag, then plant with the right foot and throw to first.

(continued)

(continued)

Technique 2
(a) Step across and to the outfield side of the bag with the left foot.

Technique 2
(b) Sweep the back corner of the bag with the right foot.

(continued)

Technique 2
(c) Come off the bag, plant with the right foot, and throw to first.

20. Footwork on a Double Play— Second Baseman

Purpose: To establish good footwork to turn a double play.

Procedure

1. Using a similar format as in **drill #19**, the players line up at the second base position and the coach (or another tosser) is positioned closer to third base.

2. A double play from the second base side can be turned in primarily two ways.

   - Technique 1 — When the fielder can reach the bag before the ball, she should wait and time her arrival so that she reaches the bag at the same time as the ball. (The fielder will be on the shortstop side of second base.) She puts her left foot on the bag and reaches out toward the ball *(a)*. After catching it, she steps off the bag, plants her right foot on the shortstop side of the bag, and throws to first *(b)*.

   - Technique 2 — When the fielder reaches the bag late, she should position herself on the first base side of second base. She then steps on second with her left foot *(a)*, pushes back away from the bag, plants with the right foot, and throws to first *(b)*.

3. Each fielder makes 5-10 plays.

Key Points

- The first time the players attempt the footwork, they should do so without a ball. Next, have them do the footwork receiving the ball only. Then progress to actually throwing the ball to first base. (You will need to add a receiver at first.)

- The players must receive the ball with both hands up asking for the ball. No matter what, be sure to get the out at second base before throwing to first.

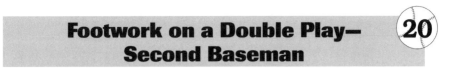

Technique 1
(a) Place left foot on the bag and prepare to receive the ball with two hands.

Technique 1
(b) Step across the bag, then plant with the right foot and throw to first.

(continued)

(continued)

Technique 2
(a) Place left foot on the bag and receive the ball with two hands.

Technique 2
(b) Push back off of the bag, then plant with the right foot and throw to first.

Pitcher and Catcher Drills

his chapter includes drills for both ends of the "battery." **Drills #21-#27** cover the defensive techniques all pitchers need to practice, including fielding bunts, throwing to bases, covering home on wild pitches, and knocking down balls. **Drills #28-#35** focus on catcher skills, including blocking balls, fielding bunts, throwing to bases, and making plays at the plate.

Give your pitchers and catchers a significant amount of attention defensively. The pitchers need to be good defensive players and must be given time to work on their defensive skills in practice. Once an opposing team finds out the pitcher can't move, field, or throw, you can be sure they will try to exploit that weakness by hitting up the middle. Many coaches try to protect the pitcher from injury by not allowing her to compete in the standard defensive drills. I believe this philosophy can actually work to injure the player more because the player will be less familiar with, and therefore less prepared for, this type of situation when it arises in the game.

Pitchers must be able to field bunts including squeeze bunts. They also need to be able to field grounders and pop-ups that are hit into the pitching circle. They must be able to throw to all bases and understand their backup responsibilities. You should hold the same defensive expectations of the pitchers as you demand of all other positions. Allowing pitchers to practice with their teammates also contributes a great deal toward creating team chemistry.

Some teams tend to play better defensively behind some pitchers rather than others. It is important for pitchers to demonstrate their loyalty to their teammates when their teammates make mistakes rather than criticize them for costing the pitchers the game—this builds support and elevates the team's level of play.

Catchers are a critical part of the success of any team. The catcher should be one of your best players. She should have good hands so she can receive and block balls well. She should be able to get up quickly to field bunts. It is also important for the catcher to have a quick arm to keep the offensive players honest. She does not necessarily have to have a great strong arm, just a quick one. A low, one-bounce throw to second can be as effective or more effective than a loopy throw on the fly.

Look to see how long it takes the catcher to make the play from the time she receives the ball to the time it reaches second base.

There seem to be more left-handed catchers recently. Although it may not be ideal, being left handed is not a reason to eliminate a player from the catcher position. In some cases being left handed can be an advantage. When coming out to field bunts the left-handed catcher has her feet already in the proper position to throw to first base.

Physical size may also be an issue when selecting a catcher. Ideally you would like the catcher to be of good physical size for her age group so she can withstand potential collisions at the plate. You don't want a player so large, however, that she blocks out the umpire's view of the pitch. The large player must be able to make herself small when receiving the pitch. Pick the player with the greatest desire to play the position—catching is a hard, physically demanding position. I would rather have a 5'4" player with all the heart than a 5'10" player who really does not want to catch.

As with the pitchers, coaches tend to neglect the defensive skills of the catchers. **Drills #28, Blocking Balls**, and **#29, Framing Pitches**, can be done with a partner every day if need be to keep your catchers sharp. The better catchers are at blocking pitches, the more confidence the pitchers will have in throwing drop balls and other pitches. The last thing you want is for your pitchers to be afraid of throwing certain pitches because the catcher can't handle them. Make sure each catcher has adequate practice time with each of your pitchers. The pitchers need to feel comfortable with the catchers and vice versa.

Fielding Bunts—Pitchers

Purpose: To practice fielding bunts.

Procedure

1. Start with one or more pitchers in the mound area; place another pitcher or a player acting as the receiver at first base, at second base, or both, to receive the thrown ball at the bases.

2. The coach tosses a ball from home plate to in front of the mound, and the pitcher fields the bunt using the standard fielding procedure as described in **drill #7, Fielding Bunts—Corners**, and throws to first base. Remind the pitcher to surround the ball by setting her feet toward the base to which she is most likely to throw.

3. The pitcher then returns to the mound and repeats the standard bunt fielding procedure, either throwing to first again or alternating her throws to different bases.

4. Each pitcher fields and throws at least five balls to specified bases.

Key Points

- The right-handed pitcher approaches the ball and fields it off of her back (right) foot, keeping her chest directed toward first base, her back to third, and her knees bent.

- The fielding footwork for the left-handed pitcher is also important to work on. The left-hander approaches the ball and fields it off her back (left) foot, keeping her chest toward third base and her back to first. Another way to say this is to "circle the ball" before picking it up.

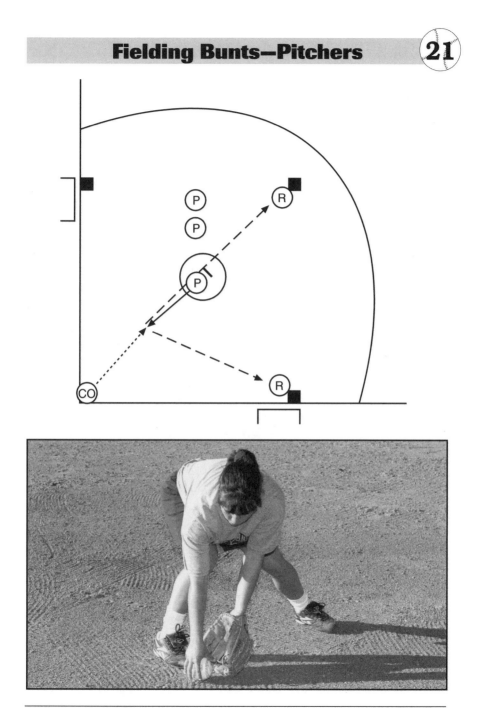

Surround the ball first, aligning the body in the direction of the throw, and pick up the ball on the back foot.

Purpose: To learn to defend the squeeze bunt with a runner on third.

Procedure

1. Start with one or more pitchers at the mound area and a coach and a catcher (or other player) acting as the receiver at home.

2. Upon recognizing a squeeze bunt, the pitcher breaks off the mound and surrounds the ball so the ball is on her throwing hand side. She then shovels the ball toward the catcher with her bare hand and the back of the glove. The ball should be tossed at knee height to the plate.

3. Each pitcher fields 10-15 bunts.

Key Points

- The offense may try to squeeze anytime they have a quick runner on third base and less than two outs.

- The pitcher should run through the ball, taking one or two steps toward home plate after releasing the ball.

Variations

- Use a real runner at third base for more gamelike practice.

- Combine this drill with **drill #8, Fielding Squeeze Bunts— Corners**, to let the whole infield practice squeeze bunts and communication at once.

23 Throwing to Bases—Pitchers

Purpose: To practice throwing to all bases.

Procedure

1. Begin with a pitcher on the mound, a person receiving throws at each base (or one person rotating through the bases), and a person hitting balls. Each pitcher should practice throwing to each of the four bases during this drill.

2. The pitcher goes through a windup without a ball, and the fungoer throws a ball in the air and then hits the ball toward the pitcher.

3. The pitcher moves to field the ball in the center of her body, fielding it as described under "Fielding" in chapter 1.

4. Each pitcher fields and throws 10 balls to each base including home.

Key Point

- The back foot must be set perpendicular to the base before throwing.

Variations

- Change the base to which the ball is to be thrown right before the pitcher throws it. She should remember to reset the feet before throwing to the new target.

- Set up a play first by placing runners at home or at any base. Use either real runners or ghost runners to simulate game situations.

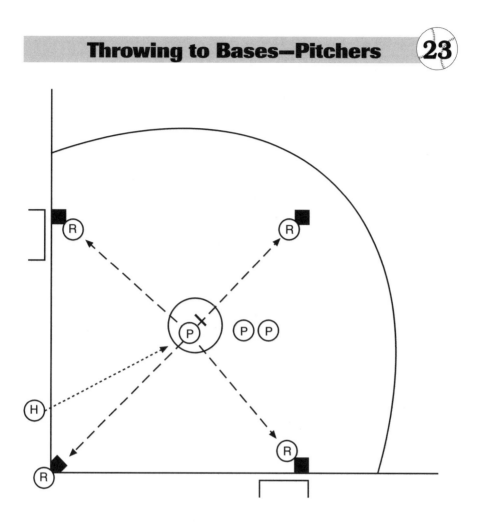

24 Run the Ball to First

Purpose: To recognize when to run the ball and toss it to first base instead of throwing it to first base. This skill is normally used when no one is on base, and the batter is not a slapper.

Procedure

1. The pitchers line up at the mound area. The coach is at home plate, and another pitcher or player receives the throws at first base.

2. The pitcher begins with a windup without a ball, and the fungoer hits balls directly at the pitcher or to the first base side of the mound.

3. When the ball is hit hard right back to the pitcher and no one is on base, the pitcher has time to run toward first base and toss it to the first baseman. She fields the ball first, then turns and runs toward first base. At the same time, she takes the ball out of her glove (hanging her throwing arm down to her side and out in front of her) with the palm of her hand behind the ball. When the pitcher gets a few feet from first base, she tosses the ball underhand to the first base receiver.

4. Hit 10-15 balls at each pitcher.

Key Points

- If the ball is not hit hard or directly at the pitcher or the pitcher bobbles the ball, she must throw the ball to first as practiced in **drill #3, Forehand Flips**.

- The pitcher should take one or two steps toward first base after she releases the ball. (We call this running through the ball.)

- If the pitcher has to move at all toward third base to field the ball, she must set her feet and throw the ball to first.

Variation

- After practicing the skill as described, hit balls to each pitcher in all directions and at different speeds to help pitchers recognize when to run the ball to first and when to throw it.

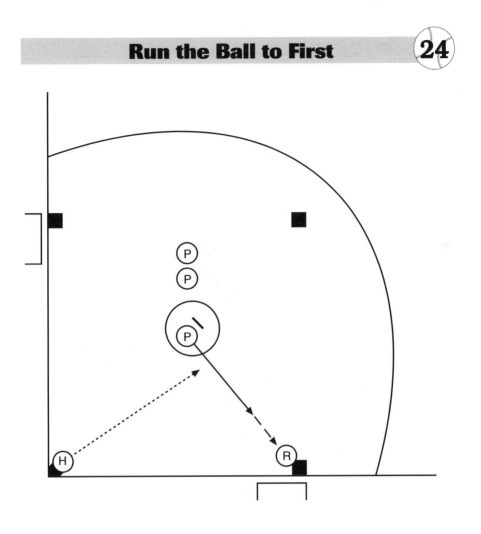

25 Plate Coverage on a Wild Pitch

Purpose: To teach pitchers proper technique for plays at the plate on passed balls or wild pitches when a runner is on third.

Procedure

1. Line pitchers up on the mound. Catchers may be used in this drill so they can practice throwing balls back to the plate, but this is not a necessity.

2. If you're using a catcher, place her in a catching stance at home plate. The coach then throws a ball to the backstop for the catcher to throw back to the plate. If no catcher is involved the coach stands at the backstop and throws balls back to the plate.

3. The pitcher runs to the plate, positioning herself on the back side of the plate if possible and up the line 1-2 feet, where she waits in a semicrouched position for the ball to be thrown.

4. The pitcher receives the ball and tags the incoming ghost runner in front of the plate.

5. Each pitcher catches 5-10 throws.

Key Point

• The pitcher may not be able to get to the back side of home plate in time for every play, but it is ideal if she can.

Variations

• This drill can be combined with **drill #31, Passed Balls and Wild Pitches**, if you prefer to work both pitchers and catchers in one drill.

• Use real runners so the pitchers can practice their timing when arriving at the plate, but have the runners slide away from the plate so no contact is made.

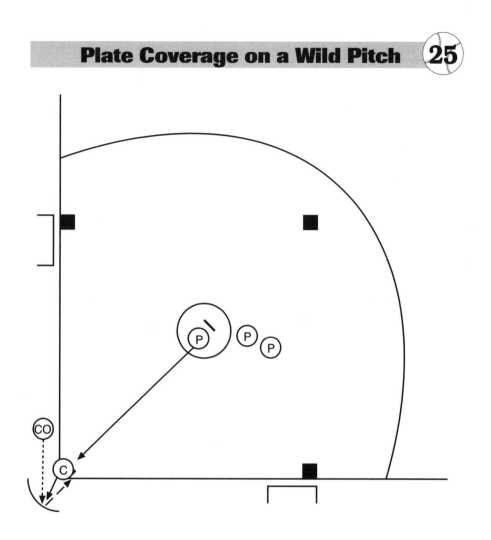

Backup Responsibilities

Purpose: To establish backup responsibilities for the pitcher. The pitcher's main backup responsibility comes when a ball is hit beyond an outfielder and a potential play is being made at either third base or home plate.

Procedure

1. Start with base runners, an outfielder, a third baseman, and a catcher, with the coach standing at the plate.

2. The coach places a base runner at first or second, then hits a ball by the outfielder, either over the player's head or in a gap.

3. The pitcher recognizes that a play will be made at either third or the plate, and she immediately sprints toward and crosses the third base foul line between third and home plate and ends up in foul territory close to dead ball territory or the dugout.

4. The pitcher turns to watch the play develop. She can cheat toward the base to which the throw is likely to go. Once she knows to which base the ball will be thrown she gets in position behind the fielder, leaving enough distance to be able to react to the overthrow (approximately 20-30 feet). On an enclosed field the pitcher is usually near the dugout or the fence line.

5. Have pitchers practice backup positions when the rest of the team is practicing relays and cutoffs (see **drill #62, Relays and Cutoffs**).

Key Point

- If the ball is overthrown it is the pitcher's responsibility to block the ball. She must prevent the ball from going out of play. Pitchers can use the down-and-block fielding technique described in chapter 1 or the technique described for fielding bad throws in **drill #18, Fielding Bad Throws**.

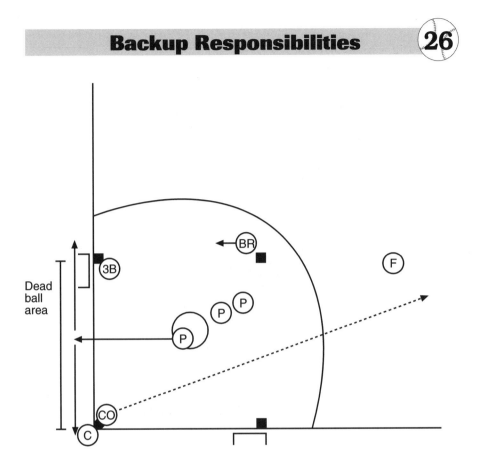

Knockdowns

Purpose: To simulate a ball hit hard back to the pitcher off her shins or elsewhere on her body.

Procedure

1. The pitchers line up at the mound area, and the first pitcher up begins about 2 feet in front of the mound, facing home plate. A receiver is at first base ready for the throw from the pitcher. A coach stands close to the pitcher with a ball.

2. The pitcher closes her eyes, and the coach gently tosses a ball off the pitcher's body.

3. The pitcher must find the ball, scoop it up with two hands, and get into position to throw to first. The pitcher surrounds the ball so it is on the back foot as when fielding a bunt.

4. Each pitcher fields 10 balls.

Key Points

- There is usually a sense of urgency in this situation; the pitcher needs to remain calm.

- When bouncing the ball off the pitcher's backside, make sure she sets her feet properly before throwing.

Variation

- While the pitcher is picking up the ball, the coach and other players can yell, creating noise to simulate the stress the pitcher would feel in an actual game situation.

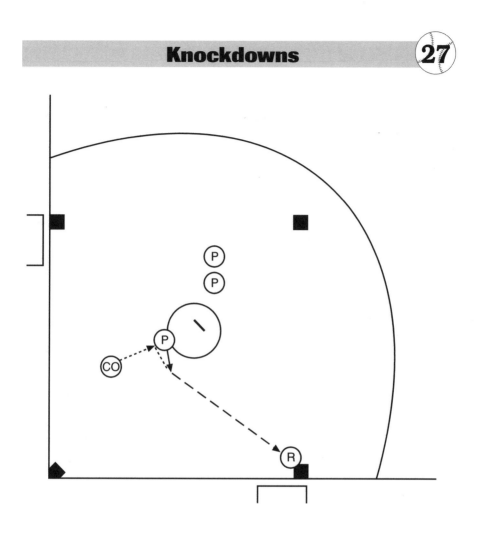

Blocking Balls

Purpose: To practice blocking low pitches or balls in the dirt. This is a key skill drill for catchers, with the benefit of providing a good conditioning element as well.

Procedure

1. Catchers can work with another catcher or a coach serving as a tosser. The catcher, in full gear, starts in the ready position for receiving a pitch. The tosser stands approximately 20 feet in front of her.
2. The tosser begins by throwing a ball in the dirt (or on the ground if working inside) directly at the catcher.
3. The catcher should drop to both knees as her glove drops, palm up, directly between her legs. Simultaneously, she should drop the chin to the chest and round the shoulders, creating an enclosure. The ball should stay in front of the catcher.
4. Each catcher blocks two sets of 5 or 10 balls.

Key Points

- Catchers must learn to actually replace the original position of their feet with their knees.
- Watch to make sure the body weight drops straight down.
- This drill can be done every day with another catcher or while catching for a pitcher.

Variations

- Add blocking balls that are one foot off the plate to each side. The catcher drops to her knees at an angle toward the ball. Then she immediately scoots her feet around the ball so she squares herself to the ball.
- Use a pitching machine to pitch balls at the catcher.
- Begin by using softie balls or Wiffle balls and progress to the harder softball.

Framing Pitches

Purpose: To teach catchers how to make more pitches look like strikes. Framing pitches does not mean pulling or yanking pitches back toward the plate; it is simply an attempt to widen the plate to increase the chance of getting the corners called as strikes.

Procedure

1. Catchers can work with another catcher or a coach. One catcher sets up in the ready position, approximately 5-6 feet from her partner.

2. If using two catchers, one player at a time throws the ball to the other. Start with only one pitch location at a time, for example, high and inside. I like to start with inside pitches because they are the easiest to frame.

3. The idea is to catch the side of the ball for inside and outside pitches and the top half of the ball for high and low pitches. On all pitches catchers should not allow the hand to move away from the plate after the ball hits the glove.

4. Throw 10 balls to each spot: high and inside, low and inside, high and outside, low and outside. Work repetitions with one pitch location at a time until mastered.

Key Points

The following descriptions are for the right-handed thrower with a right-handed batter.

- For a low pitch (not a ball in the dirt), catch the ball with the palm down *(a)*. A low pitch caught palm up almost always looks like a ball.

- For the high pitch *(b)*, catch the top half of the ball, slightly rotating the top of the glove down.

- For the inside pitch *(c)*, keep the elbow down and catch the left side of the ball, slightly squeezing the ball toward the plate.

- For the outside pitch *(d)*, quickly get the glove around the ball, backhanding the pitch.

a

b

c

d

30. Throwing to Bases—Catchers

Purpose: To practice throwing to all bases.

Procedure

1. Throws to first, second, and third base on balls fielded at the plate (like full swing bunts) or on pickoff attempts and throws to second on straight steals and in first and third situations should be covered with each catcher.

   For pickoffs at first base, the catcher(s) are at home plate, a pitcher or coach is on the mound, and a first and second baseman are in their respective positions. Usually on a pickoff at first with a runner on first, the first baseman acts as a decoy and gets out of the way as the second baseman sneaks in behind the runner who has taken a big lead. The catcher then throws the ball on the inside of first base to the waiting second baseman *(a)*. Do the same for pickoffs at third, only the third baseman usually takes the throws from the catcher when attempting to pick off the runner at third. The throw to third should be directly to the base.

   To practice throws for straight steals, begin with a line of runners at first base and a shortstop at second base to receive the throws *(b)*. Have the runners practice getting leads and sliding at second base. The throws to second should be low and slightly up the line. It is also helpful to put a batter in the batter's box.

2. A coach or player pitches a ball from the mound area to the catcher in ready position wearing full gear at home plate.

3. Begin by setting up each situation and executing the plays four or five times with no runners. Next, add runners and repeat the plays for an additional four to five throws.

Key Point

- As with any throwing drill, the key action is all in the feet. Players must ensure that their feet are positioned properly for each throw.

a

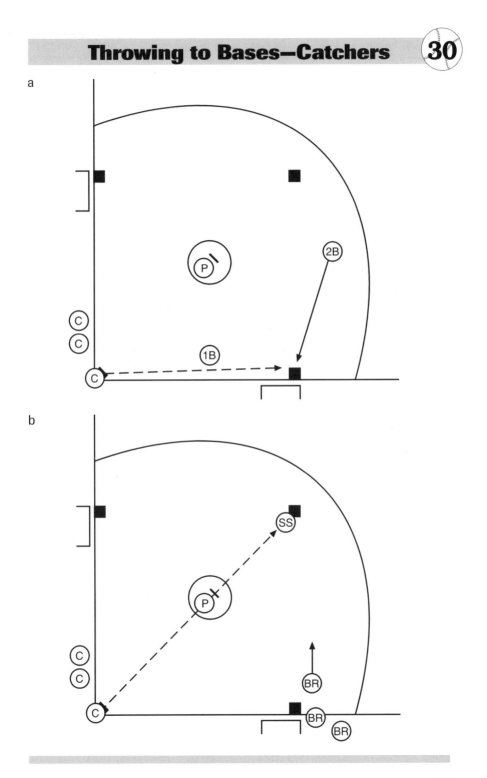

b

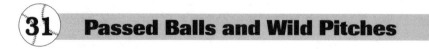

Purpose: To practice getting to the ball quickly and accurately and throwing it back to the plate.

Procedure

1. The catcher starts in a ready position at home plate in full gear. A coach is in front of the catcher and throws a ball behind the catcher, simulating a wild pitch. The coach can take the throw from the catcher or use a pitcher.

2. The catcher throws off her mask in the direction opposite the ball (to avoid tripping over it) and runs back to the backstop, surrounding the ball so that her throwing arm is closest to the backstop. As she approaches the ball, she should fall to her knees and slide toward it.

3. Using the back of her glove as a brace, the catcher picks the ball up with the bare hand and sidearm throws the ball back to the plate. The ball should be thrown about 1-2 feet up the line and at knee height.

4. Each catcher makes 10 throws.

Key Point

- Use the sidearm throw with the back bent forward to keep the ball down. The catcher shouldn't stand up to throw back to the plate.

Variations

- Add other positions to the drill for various base coverage and backup responsibilities. For example, in a game you may have the pitcher cover home plate, or you may have the first baseman cover it. If not receiving the ball, either the first or third baseman should back up the throw.

- Rather than throwing the ball to the backstop, the drill can start with the ball already placed at the backstop.

- Combine this drill with **#25, Plate Coverage on a Wild Pitch**, for pitchers and catchers to practice this skill at the same time.

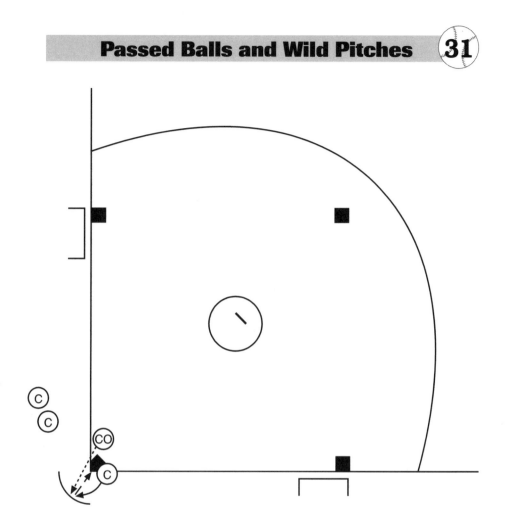

Tag Plays at the Plate

Purpose: To develop the proper set-up position to receive the ball and take a collision with the runner attempting to score.

Procedure

1. The catcher sets up 1-2 feet up the third base foul line. The catcher's feet must be facing the direction from which the ball is being thrown. The left foot is close to the third base foul line, taking away most of the plate.

2. The coach throws balls to the plate on one bounce from the mound or a little deeper. As the catcher receives the ball, she begins to square her body toward third base with her feet facing third. Her knees must be bent.

3. In a game situation, if the runner slides, the catcher simultaneously receives the ball and begins to go down on both knees to tag the runner with two hands to prevent the ball from being knocked out. If the runner tries to avoid the tag by sliding to the back of the plate, the catcher must take her hands to the plate for the tag. She doesn't try to chase the runner—the runner must come to the plate to be safe.

4. Each catcher takes 5-10 throws.

Key Points

- Make sure the catcher is square to third base and her knees are bent. This will prevent any knee injuries caused by the knees being hit from the side.

- The catcher should not be blocking the plate if she does not have the ball.

Variation

- To simulate a collision, the coach can hold a football tackling pad or a similar padded object and collide with the catcher. Using padding allows the coach to safely demonstrate to the catchers how to take the impact of the runner.

Fielding Bunts—Catchers

Purpose: To develop proper footwork to ensure a quick release and an accurate throw.

Procedure

1. The catcher begins in a ready position, and a receiver is at the designated base. Start with throws to first base, then second, and finally third. The coach is in the batter's box and drops balls out in front of the plate to simulate bunts.

2. The catcher identifies where the ball has been bunted and begins to surround the ball. She should not run directly at the ball. Instead, she surrounds the ball in the direction of the base on which the play will be made so that she fields the ball at her back foot. The back foot is perpendicular to the target. For example, if the ball is bunted toward the first base side and the throw is going to first, the catcher comes out and begins to turn her back to third and position herself so the ball is at her back foot and both her feet are pointing toward the first base foul line.

3. Once the body is in position, the catcher fields the bunt with both hands and makes the throw. She may use the back of her glove to stop the spin and scoop the ball.

4. Each catcher fields 10 bunts in various areas.

Key Points

- Throws to first should be chest high to the inside of the first base bag; throws to second and third base should be chest high directly over the bag.
- If the catcher surrounds the ball and is set up to throw to one base and changes her mind, she must reset her feet so her back foot is perpendicular to the new target.

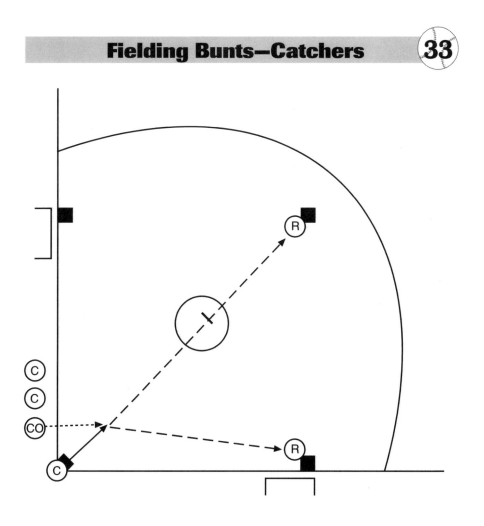

34 Pop-Ups—Catchers

Purpose: To practice catching pop-ups behind or to the side of home plate.

Procedure

1. The catcher begins in a ready position. The coach stands in front of the catcher and throws the ball in the air.
2. Once the ball is thrown, the catcher first identifies in which direction the ball has been hit (or thrown in this drill). She then throws her mask in the opposite direction, so she will not later trip, and makes the catch.
3. Each catcher catches 10 pop-ups in various areas.

Key Points

- As she goes to catch the ball, the catcher should turn her glove so that her thumb is parallel to the ground. She should catch the ball using both hands at her chest, not above or equal with her head.
- If the ball is behind the catcher, and she has time, she should turn her back to the infield.
- If the ball is in front or to the side of her, the catcher should stay facing the infield and use the normal fielding technique.

Variations

- The coach may actually fungo balls in the air.
- The coach can use a pitching machine to simulate pop-ups.

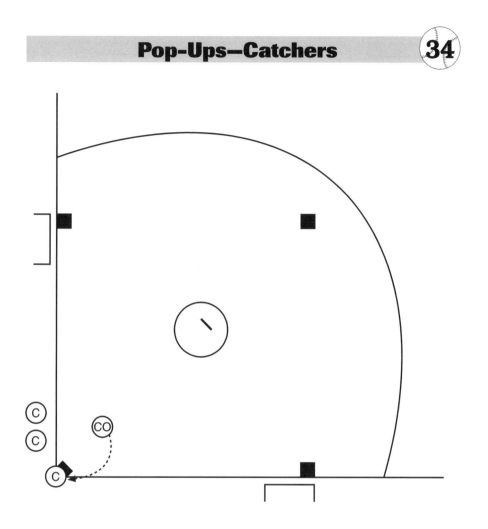

Intentional Walks

Purpose: To be prepared for the intentional walk situation.

Procedure

1. A lined catcher's box is needed for this drill. A pitcher can also practice intentional walks at this time or a coach can pitch.

2. The catcher sets up standing behind the plate but in the batter's box opposite the batter. The catcher can then indicate the target at her chest with the glove hand.

3. Once the ball leaves the pitcher's hand, the catcher may step out of the catcher's box.

4. Practice two or three walks on both sides of the plate.

Key Points

- The catcher must set up with both feet in the box.

- If runners are on base, the catcher should immediately set her feet for a throw after the ball is caught in case runners attempt to advance.

- Practice this drill with the entire infield to go over backups in case of a wild pitch, or throws if a runner tries to advance.

With a right-handed
batter, the catcher sets up
on right side of box and steps
out after pitch.

4

Outfielder Drills

T his chapter includes drills to practice every outfield defensive situation, including grounders, routine and deep fly balls, line drives, and throwing correctly from the outfield. The outfield is a vital part of the defense at all levels — don't neglect any of the basic fundamentals listed in chapter 6.

Outfielders are the last line of defense. In the early stages of a player's career, the toughest challenge you may face as a coach is convincing the player how important playing the outfield truly is. No one thinks playing the outfield is very important until that one routine ground ball goes through someone's legs for a home run, a situation we've all been in at one time or another. Playing the outfield is a mentally demanding position. Whereas the infielders play knowing that someone is always behind them backing them up, the outfielders know they are the team's last line of defense. In addition, many innings can go by without an outfielder getting a ball, and then they get that one chance to save the game, catching that ball in the seventh inning with the winning run on second base. The only way the outfielders are really going to believe the position is important is if the coach ensures adequate outfield practice time. This can be a special challenge for those of us who train indoors, but by looking through the drill finder you will find that some of the outfield drills in this book can be used indoors.

Ideally, outfielders should have good foot speed, a better than average throwing arm, the ability to judge fly balls, and the willingness to dive. Some players just do not have good depth perception. The coach can easily find out which players have good depth perception by hitting fly balls to the players under consideration. Some players make up for their lack of foot speed by getting an excellent jump on the ball. Players who have excellent foot speed can get away with misjudging balls because they can make up for this with speed. Either ability can work on its own. The best situation, however, is to have a player who gets great jumps on the balls and is quick at the same time.

When picking which positions players should play, put all of them in left field and hit balls; do the same in the right field. You will be able to tell which players tend to see the ball off the bat better depending on which field they are in. Usually, the left-handed player plays right or center field. I usually put my quickest player in center field since she'll have the most ground to cover.

The outfielders should always set up square to the batter. Overadjusting with one foot significantly (more than six inches) in front of the other isn't worth the risk of getting a slow start if the ball goes in the other direction. On intermediate and advanced teams, the outfielders should be signaled what pitch is going to be thrown so they can make small adjustments in their positions accordingly. For example, if the pitcher is going to throw a change-up, the outfielders should all shift two to four steps to the hitter's pull side. In the case of a curve ball from a right-handed pitcher to a right-handed batter, the outfielders should all shift two to four steps toward right field. Potential slappers also should be played differently. If a slapper cannot hit with power, the outfielders should move in a few steps. If the slapper tends to run out of the box toward first base, the left fielder can play in even closer.

It is important for outfielders to remember how each batter hit in previous innings and make adjustments. Coaches and players should not, however, make major adjustments (over one step) without a good reason. Play in a straight, normal position if there is no solid information about the hitter.

Outfielders should also alert the middle infielders to major shifts in positioning. For example, when the opponent's fourth hitter comes up and the outfielders know she pulls the ball deep, the left fielder will take several steps back and one or two steps toward the foul line and yell to the shortstop, "Hey, I'm back." This reminds the shortstop that she may have to run back and make a play on a short fly to left.

Take the time in practice to go over each outfielder's backup responsibilities. The outfielder has a place to be on every hit. Every ball hit to an infielder should be backed up by an outfielder as if there were no infielders. The outfielders must also back up each other—even the most routine balls can be missed. Many times outfielders can get lulled into not paying attention. They must force themselves to be involved on every pitch.

Fly Balls—Partner Toss

Purpose: To learn to stay back on a fly ball and develop momentum into the throw.

Procedure

1. The outfielder starts on the left field foul line facing fair territory, and another player (or the coach) stands approximately 5-10 feet slightly in front and to the side of the fielder. A third player stands directly across from the outfielder approximately 100-150 feet away and is the receiver of the throw.

2. The partner or coach tosses the ball in front of the fielder, high enough so that she has time to set up.

3. After the ball is tossed, the outfielder turns sideways with her feet at a 45-degree angle to the throwing target, left foot in front of right (for right-handers). The fielder brings her hands up, turning the glove slightly sideways so her thumb is parallel to the ground, and places her throwing hand on the side of the glove. The object is to set up the body to throw so when the ball is caught the player can throw quickly.

4. The fielder should stay behind the ball, wait for it to come down, catch the ball on her throwing side, and throw to the receiver.

5. Toss five balls to each fielder, then switch so the receiver is the fielder. Repeat twice.

Key Points

- The fielder must let the ball come down below her eyes.
- The fielder should catch the ball with both hands and make the throw in one smooth motion, like infielders do when running through the ball as they field on the charge.

Variation

- Have all of your outfielders line up at the foul line and rotate up one at a time. One player acting as a receiver stands 100-150 feet away. Each player rotates through to make five catches and throws.

Sun Balls

Purpose: To learn to catch a fly ball when playing in sunny conditions.

Procedure

1. Before the drill begins, each fielder should identify the sun's position. Fielders should put their gloves up slightly sideways and closed to shield their eyes from the sun. This will prepare them for the drill. This preparation also needs to be done in the game on sunny days.

2. Fielders can set up anywhere in the outfield where there is room. A partner tosses a ball in the air directly into the sun, and the outfielder holds up her glove as described in step 1.

3. If a fielder loses the ball in the sun she must look down and try to pick up the ball as it comes out of the sun.

4. Toss five balls and switch roles. Repeat twice.

Key Points

- Do this drill on a sunny day.
- Outfielders must learn to position themselves so that they are not looking directly at the sun ball but are instead using peripheral vision to locate it.
- Outfielders should wear visors when necessary.

Variations

- Start with partner tosses and then hit fly balls to each fielder.
- Run the drill with two outfielders in position. Hit sun balls between the two to help them learn to communicate when one player has a better line on the ball. The player whose vision is less blocked by the sun should catch the ball if possible and, at minimum, give directions to help her fellow outfielder to locate the ball and make the catch.
- The outfielders line up and rotate through one at a time while the coach tosses pop-ups.

Purpose: To teach outfielders to run to a spot and then find the ball. This skill is used for balls that the player immediately knows are over her head but that she can still catch. This drill includes a good conditioning element as well.

Procedure

1. Outfielders form a line at one of the starting positions (e.g., everyone lines up in left field). One outfielder is up at a time, and a coach is in front of the fielder. Prior to tossing the ball the coach picks a spot to the left or the right of the player, approximately 30 feet behind her, and shows the spot to the player. This spot should be within the range of a sprinting outfielder.

2. When the coach tosses the ball to the designated spot the player puts her head down (taking her eyes off the ball) and sprints to the spot she thinks the ball will be. Next, she turns to find the ball and catches it.

3. Toss 8-10 balls to a spot to the left of each outfielder and then repeat to the right.

Key Points

- Once an outfielder knows the ball is hit over her head, she must turn and sprint to the spot (with her head down), then look up to find the ball. Make sure the fielder looks for the ball early but not so early that she tracks the ball the entire way.

- The fielder should not run directly under the ball; she should try to keep it to one side or the other.

Variations

- Practice in all three outfield positions.
- The coach fungos balls from home plate or the pitcher's mound area.
- Practice the drill near the fence. If there is a fence to deal with the fielder should get to the fence first then find the ball. This is an advanced skill.

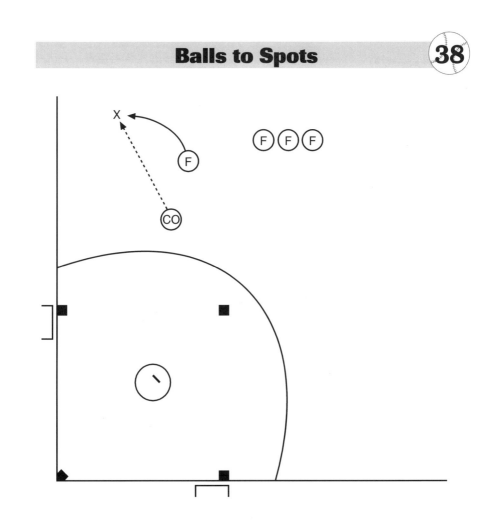

Purpose: To learn to catch a fly ball on or near the home run fence.

Procedure

1. The outfielder begins in a ready position approximately 15-20 yards from the outfield fence.
2. A coach or partner stands 20-30 feet in front of the player with a ball and throws the ball up and over the player's head.
3. The fielder turns, puts her head down, and runs to the fence. She finds the fence with her throwing arm (by touching the fence) and stays sideways to be able to move quickly one way or the other, then turns to find the ball and makes the catch.
4. Each fielder catches 5-10 balls.

Key Points

- The fielder's starting position in the outfield should be the distance the player can cover in a full sprint to reach the fence before the batted ball.
- When the outfielder knows the ball is hit near the outfield fence, she must find the fence first then pick up the ball.
- If possible, the outfielder should always go into the fence with her throwing arm to cushion the impact of the fence and to help keep the ball in the glove.
- If the ball is above the outfielder's head, she should get to the fence first and jump vertically to avoid injury.

Variation

- A coach or partner can hit balls from the mound area.

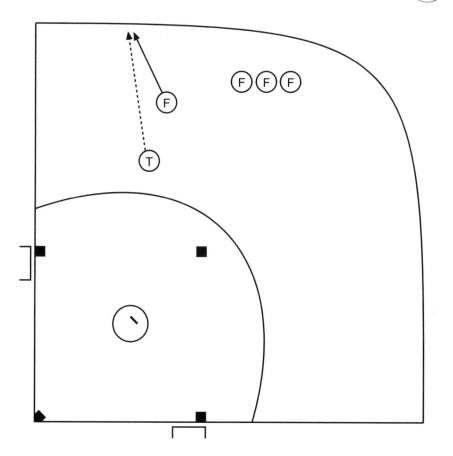

40 **Sliding to the Foul Line Fence**

Purpose: To learn to slide into the foul line fence to catch a fly ball.

Procedure

1. The outfielders form a line in right or left field. The tosser stands in foul territory, within 2-3 feet of the foul line fence.

2. The tosser says, "Go," and the player sprints toward the fence; as the player approaches, the tosser throws up a ball 2-3 feet off the fence.

3. The player does a bent leg slide into the fence under the ball. The legs should be relaxed to act as shock absorbers. The arms stay down and the ball is caught in the gut with the glove and palm facing up (like a basket catch).

4. Each fielder catches 5-10 balls.

Key Points

• Never dive headfirst into the fence.

• This technique, although primarily used by outfielders, can be used by all players who may chase a ball into foul territory, whether into a fence or a dugout.

• Make sure players keep their legs relaxed to cushion the impact.

Variations

• Have players practice running and sliding into the fence without a ball before adding the tosser.

• Fungo the ball from the mound.

• To practice this drill indoors, use any wall with a smooth surface as the "fence" and a smooth floor in front of it. Place a sliding mat up against the wall to prevent injury.

Crow Hop

Purpose: To develop more power in the outfielder's throw and prolong the life of the throwing arm.

Procedure

1. Set up as in **drill #36, Fly Balls—Partner Toss**. The partner tosses the ball in front of the fielder, high enough so that she has time to set up.

2. After the ball is tossed, the outfielder turns sideways with her feet at a 45-degree angle to the throwing target, left foot in front of right (for right-handers). The fielder brings her hands up, turning the glove slightly sideways so the thumb is parallel to the ground, and places the throwing hand on the side of the glove. The object is to set up the body to throw so when the ball is caught the player can throw quickly.

3. The fielder should stay behind the ball, wait for it to come down, and catch the ball on her throwing side. Immediately after the outfielder catches the ball, she should lift her right knee, pushing up and forward in a motion similar to an exaggerated skip. She turns her body sideways in midair and lands with her right foot perpendicular to the target. At the same time, the outfielder brings her arm down to her side in the basic overhand throwing technique (see chapter 1). As she releases the ball, she bends her back and falls forward.

4. Each fielder catches and throws 5-10 balls, depending on how much other throwing is done on that practice day.

Key Points

- The fielder should "break her back" when she throws, allowing her upper body to bend at the waist so her chest is parallel to the ground.
- The fielder should get rid of the ball as quickly as possible.

Variation

- Fungo balls at the players, hitting grounders in addition to fly balls.

Throw to Trash Can

Purpose: To develop accurate throws to bases. This drill emphasizes keeping the ball low and using one hop.

Procedure

1. Begin with outfielders in their positions. Place a large trash can on its side at home plate, with the open end facing the outfield.
2. From the edge of the grass, toss grounders and fly balls to the outfielders. The outfielder fields the ball and throws it into the can on one hop (if possible).
3. Outfielders field and throw 10-15 balls each; the total can vary depending on how much other throwing will be done that practice session.

Key Points

- The throw should ideally bounce once (more bounces if necessary) and stay low. The players should bend at the waist and exaggerate the follow-through when throwing the ball.
- Move the can so it is facing the direction from which the ball is being thrown.

Variations

- Place the can at various bases.
- Have outfielders create a point system to add competition. Encourage them to use their imaginations.
- Fungo balls from home plate or the pitcher's mound area.

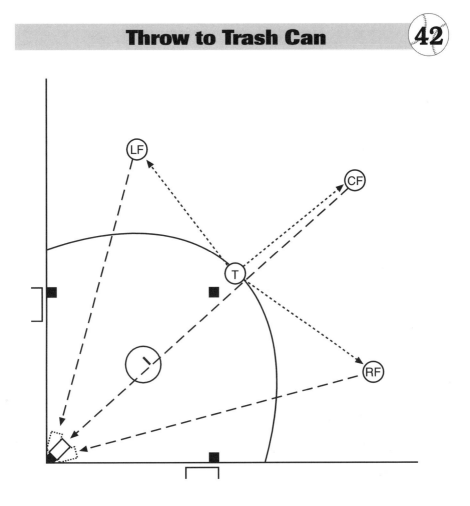

43 Momentum Into the Throw

Purpose: To teach use of the total body, staying back, and moving into the ball.

Procedure

1. A tosser stands 5 feet in front of a fielder. Another player stands 50-100 feet from the fielder and acts as a target.
2. The tosser begins by throwing a ball straight up in the air directly in front of the fielder.
3. The fielder stays back and waits for the ball to come down, then catches the ball while moving forward and throws to the target all in one motion.
4. Each player throws 5-8 balls.

Key Points

- As much as possible, outfielders should set their bodies to throw before the ball comes down to minimize the time it takes to get rid of the ball once they catch it.
- The fielder should catch the ball below her eyes, close to her throwing shoulder.

44. Balls in Position

Purpose: To develop communication among outfielders and to practice fielding fly balls and grounders.

Procedure

1. Place the outfielders in their appropriate positions. A fungoer will hit from home or near the pitcher's mound.

2. The fungoer hits fly balls and grounders in between each fielder *(a)*. One fielder calls the ball, and the other moves to back her up. The fielders can either toss the balls into a bucket or throw them back to a receiver.

3. Perform for 10-15 minutes or until adequate repetitions are completed.

Key Points

- Stress communication. Once an outfielder calls the ball, she must catch it.

- Generally the center fielder has priority in taking balls.

- Do not let outfielders look at each other after the ball has been hit. They should rely instead on listening to the other fielders to determine who will catch the ball. Many times, if players look at each other once the ball has been hit the ball ends up dropping without anyone going for it.

Variation

- Add the infielders and practice short pop-ups between the infield and the outfield *(b)*. Infielders should go for every ball unless they hear an outfielder call them off. Outfielders have priority on all balls hit between infielders and outfielders.

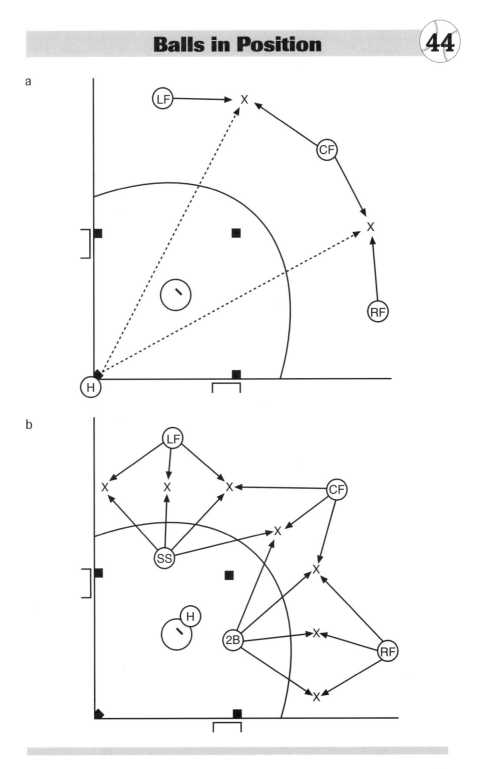

a

b

Ten-Ball Drill

Purpose: To improve concentration and practice higher repetitions in fielding fly balls. This drill supplies a strong conditioning element.

Procedure

1. One outfielder is up at a time in any space available (need one field only). A coach or player hitting or tossing balls faces the fielder. The hitter has a minimum of 10 balls ready. Another player is helpful to hand the fungoer the balls; the other outfielders waiting for their turns can be used in this role.

2. Hit fly balls to a fielder in succession, giving the fielder just enough time to catch the ball and immediately toss it out of the way before fielding the next hit. Hit a combination of short, easy fly balls and long fly balls to both sides of the fielder.

3. Hit the fielder 10 balls in a row then switch players. Do two sets of 10 for each player.

Key Points

• The fielder must get rid of the ball quickly.

• The outfielder looks for the next ball as soon as she catches the previous one.

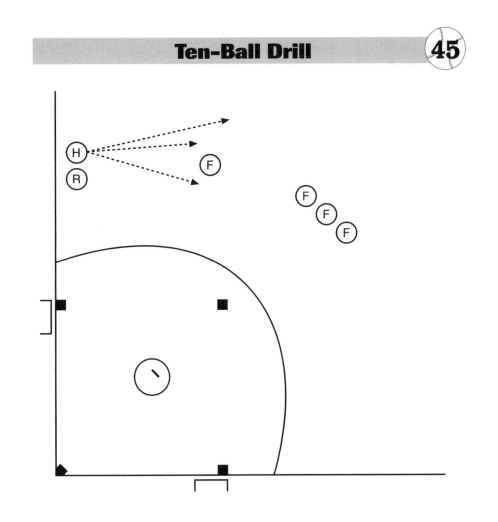

Shoestring Catches

Purpose: To catch balls hit in front of the outfielder. This drill contains a good conditioning element as well.

Procedure

1. Place players in two lines of four or more, approximately 60 feet across from each other. The first player in one line and the second player in the other line have a ball.

2. The first player in the line where the second player has the ball runs toward the first player with the ball in the other line. When the running player comes within 10 feet of the player with the ball, the player with the ball tosses it so the player running at her must reach down and catch the ball at her shoestrings. The ball should be thrown below the knees.

3. The player who tossed the ball sprints at the player with the ball in the other line. The player who caught the ball hands it off to the next person in line and then goes to the end of the line.

4. Repeat so each player catches five balls.

Key Points

- It is important that the player's head is down when catching the ball.
- The fielder must keep her glove low to the ground and come up if the ball bounces, not the other way around.

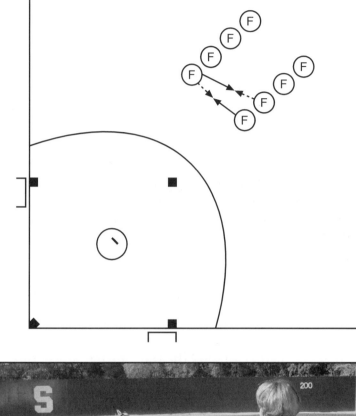

Line Drives

Purpose: To teach outfielders how to react to balls hit directly at them. The line drive may be the hardest ball for outfielders to catch.

Procedure

1. Position players in a line in the outfield. A fungo hitter stands at home plate or by the pitcher's mound area.

2. Fungo balls directly at the first player. Hit them mostly on a line, although some may have a little loft to them. These balls are hard to judge with depth perception because they are hit directly at the player.

3. The player makes the catch and throws the ball to a receiver standing by the hitter, or she tosses the ball into a bucket.

4. Each player catches 15-20 balls.

Key Points

- Teach the players not to move at first until they are certain the ball is either in front of them or behind them. The player should immediately turn sideways so that once she decides on the direction of the ball she can move quickly. It is better for the player to be sure of the ball's direction first, rather than taking three steps in before realizing the ball is over her head.

- The outfielders in line should yell "In!" or "Back!" to the player who is up. The outfielders in line can easily see where the ball is because of their angle to the ball.

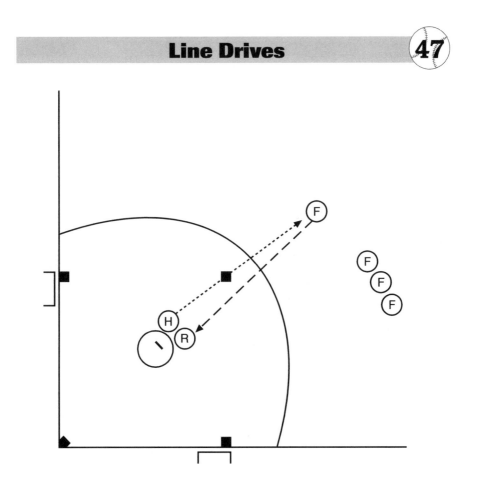

Team Drills

Expect your team to play like they practice. Plan every aspect of practice to replicate game situations as closely as possible. I like to plan practice to be slightly harder than the games. Be consistent in your practice intensity every day. Players can and will adapt to almost any coaching style.

My philosophy has always been to teach the players everything I know in practice and then let them play during games. I want my players to feel relaxed and confident at game time; once they start playing in a game, I try not to tinker with their mechanics. I use a few code words that we have established in practice that can help the players in game situations such as, "focus," "stay short," "be quick," and so on.

The softball skills and strategies that tend to be the most difficult to learn are the ones that arise when a defensive play breaks down. Have you ever coached a team that completes first and third situations (one example of many) perfectly in practice over and over, but then the players act like they don't know what to do with the ball when one throw is a little off in a game? This is what happens when players understand the skills needed for each drill but haven't developed a complete understanding of the game. To help players learn the game, have them *completely finish* all of the plays in intra-squad scrimmages and while practicing situation drills like **Controlled Fungo (drill #66)**. Since some balls are likely to be misthrown in practice, playing each situation out will help your team learn what to do when a play doesn't happen perfectly in a game. Learning when to hold a ball to minimize the damage can be as important as knowing when and where to throw it. It's also important to stress "taking care" of the ball during drills and scrimmages. Players sometimes get so caught up in making the play that they forget to catch the ball!

I also watch warm-ups carefully to emphasize the importance of correct throwing mechanics and to be in touch with how sore players' arms are from day to day. Many drills can be adapted for more or less throwing as needed. We warm up slowly and throw during every practice to keep each player's arm in shape. But remember, there are times to rest the arm so it has time to recover. We will also take time off from throwing in the off-season.

Being able to come together as a team is what a successful defense is all about. The drills in this chapter are organized from general team skills—such as throwing, basic fielding, and quickness—to putting it all together with team defensive situation drills like relays and cutoffs and controlled fungo. The players need to understand the importance of each individual working as hard as possible on her own individual skills so the entire team will be stronger when they come together. Softball is similar to an individual sport in many ways, and yet the team is only as good as its weakest player. Peer pressure can be useful when applied with the purpose of team building in mind. Many times, if you intend to punish a player in some way for making avoidable mental errors (extra laps, for example), it is okay to include the entire team. Instill in your players the team attitude that "we win together and we lose together."

48 # Basketball Spins

Purpose: To teach four-seam rotation, wrist snap, and to emphasize spinning the ball when throwing. Ideally, the ball should rotate (or spin) through the air as many times as possible once it has been thrown.

Procedure

1. Players can stand anywhere on the field or in the practice area indoors. The player starts by gripping the ball on the seams using the pads of the fingertips, as described in "Catching and Throwing" in chapter 1.

2. The player lifts the ball over her head as if to shoot a basketball. Her elbow should be pointing forward, her wrist should be cocked at 90 degrees, and the back of her hand should be parallel to the ground.

3. The player then spins the ball toward the sky, trying for as many rotations as possible. She should follow through with her wrist so the palm ends up facing down.

4. Each player spins the ball straight up 10 times.

Variations

- Allow younger players to sit or kneel to do the spins.
- Use 11-inch balls for players with small hands as a learning tool.

One-Knee Throwing

Purpose: To teach proper overhand throwing technique and to strengthen the arm.

Procedure

1. Form two lines of players directly across from each other, approximately 10 feet apart. The players should be down on one knee, with the glove-side knee up.

2. The player with the ball grips the ball as in **drill #48, Basketball Spins**, and begins by bringing the ball down, brushing her thumb across her outer midthigh. Simultaneously, she points her glove hand toward the target while opening her shoulders (a). When bringing the ball up behind the body the thrower extends the throwing arm in a line that connects the glove hand (which is extended toward the target), the opened shoulders, and the ball in the throwing hand.

3. Once the ball is behind the body in the straight line described in step 2, the player cocks her wrist and points the ball in the opposite direction of where she is throwing (b). If the player turns her head to look at her throwing hand she should see the back of her hand. Then the player brings her arm forward, leading with the elbow.

4. After releasing the ball the player should follow through so that her wrist relaxes after snapping the ball and her arm falls to the opposite hip (c).

5. Players throw for 2-3 minutes.

Key Point

- Players should be able to play catch on one knee without making any overthrows.

Variations

- Increase the distance between players to a maximum of 60 feet to strengthen the arm.

- While the players are closer together use no gloves to focus on catching with two hands.

a

b

c

50. Overhand Throwing

Purpose: To practice overhand throwing.

Procedure

1. Players set up with a partner and stand facing each other, about 15-20 feet apart, and practice overhand throws using the grip and throwing motion as described in chapter 1 and **drills #48, Basketball Spins**, and **#49, One-Knee Throwing**. Each player provides a target in the chest area for her partner, using her glove and throwing hand.

2. The receiver stands on the balls of her feet, with her feet shoulder-width apart. She moves her feet to receive the ball as close to the throwing side of her body as possible. The receiver uses two hands to catch the ball to ensure a quick release and better grip. As she catches the ball, the receiver turns her body so that her back foot is perpendicular to the target. No matter how the player catches the ball, she must set her back foot and turn her body before throwing.

3. Throw for 3 minutes and work up to 5 minutes of throwing before each practice.

Key Points

- Overhand throwing is the single most important softball skill to practice. Players should practice throwing (both kneeling and standing) for a total of 5-8 minutes each practice session.

- Players should make few if any overthrows during warm-ups.

Variations

- Have the receiver vary the target, making it high or low on different throws. The thrower must hit the target. Hit the target three times before moving on.

- Increase the distance between players to a maximum of 100 feet for strengthening of the arm.

Diamond Drill

Purpose: To help fielders improve lateral movement. This drill provides a good conditioning element as well.

Procedure

1. Players set up with a partner and stand facing each other approximately 6-10 feet apart. One player has a ball, and her partner begins in her infield ready position (outfielders can use a middle infield ready position).
2. The partner rolls the ball to the fielder's side, and the fielder responds by shuffling her feet to move to field the ball (as opposed to making a crossover step).
3. After fielding the ball with both hands the fielder immediately tosses the ball in the air back to her partner, and the partner then rolls the ball to the fielder's other side.
4. Perform this for two or three sets of 10 or 15 tosses.

Key Points

- The fielder must keep her knees bent, buttocks down, and shuffle her feet rather than doing a crossover step to get to the ball.
- Tossers should be sure to roll the ball quickly from side to side so that the fielders can work on making quick movements to each side.

Variations

- The tosser uses two balls to increase the speed at which she can roll balls to the fielder, requiring the fielder to increase her quickness in fielding the balls.
- Do this drill with or without gloves to also practice fielding with both hands.

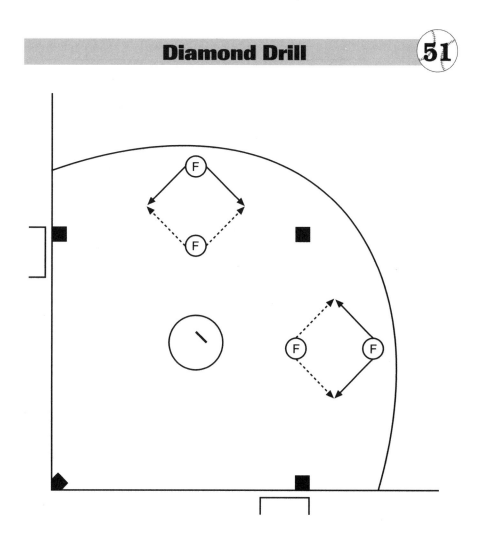

Purpose: To practice catching any ball hit over a player's head. This drill is used for all positions and provides a good conditioning element as well.

Procedure

1. Players form a line behind the coach. Each player has a ball and gives it to the coach when it is her turn.

2. The player stands facing the coach, and the coach indicates to the player (by pointing) on which side of the player the coach will throw the ball. The player drop steps in that direction, turns, and runs straight back, looking back over her shoulder to the side from which the ball is coming.

3. Once the player starts to run the coach throws a fly ball over the player's head on the side that the coach had indicated. The fielder should look back at the ball by just turning her head, not twisting her whole body, while continuing to run to make the catch. The fielder should not open up and directly face the ball; she must stay sideways so she can adjust in or out if she's misjudged the ball and then make the catch at the side of her body.

4. Throw two to three balls to each side of the player.

Key Points

- The player must keep the ball to her side and not let it pass directly over her head.
- Throw the ball high enough and far enough to make it a realistic challenge for the player.
- Throw the ball a little farther for the faster, more skilled players.

Variation

- After the player drop steps, switch the direction from which the ball is coming while the player runs. The player needs to be able to change directions without breaking stride or opening up her body toward the ball.

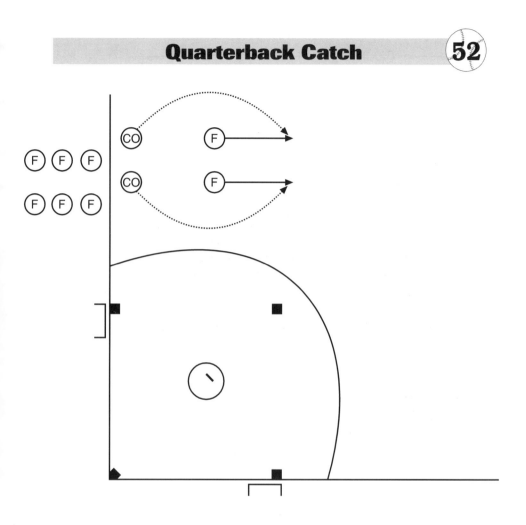

53. Short Hop/Quarterback Catch

Purpose: To work on soft hands during a catch and going back on balls over the head. This drill provides a strong conditioning element.

Procedure

1. Two players stand approximately 60 feet apart. One player stands on one of the foul lines; the other player stands around the second base area.

2. The player out in the field starts with one ball. The player on the foul line runs toward the player with the ball. The player with the ball tosses a short hop to the player running toward her. The player catches the short hop, "giving" with the ball using soft hands, and then hands the ball back to the player in the middle of the field and sprints past her.

3. The player with the ball then throws a high, long pop-up toss over the head of the runner, like in **drill #52, Quarterback Catch**. The runner catches the ball, stops, and tosses the ball back to the player in the middle. The runner then runs back toward the middle player, fields another short hop, and repeats the drill in the opposite direction.

4. Do one or two sets of five.

Key Points

- The partner must throw the pop-ups high enough to allow the fielder to get to it.
- The players should sprint to catch the pop-up.

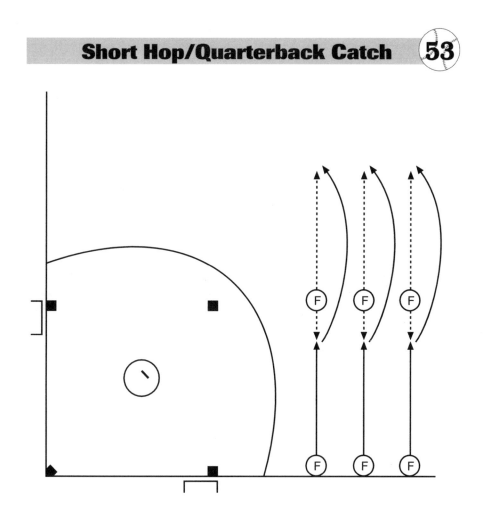

Around the Horn

Purpose: To develop quick hands, quick feet, and throwing accuracy.

Procedure

1. Start with one or more players at each base. The player at home begins with the ball.

2. The player at first base faces the plate and calls for the ball, yelling, "One, one, one!" and the player at home throws the ball to first base. If the ball is thrown to the inside of the base, the right-handed receiver does a 180-degree quick hop, turning toward the inside of the infield and setting up to throw to second base. If the ball is thrown toward the outside of the base, the receiver should turn her back toward the infield and set up to throw to second.

3. The ball is thrown around the bases. Players should pivot based on where the ball is thrown, as described for the first baseman.

4. When the ball gets back to home plate, continue around or switch directions. Throw the ball around the bases for 4-8 minutes.

Key Points

- Execute the drill as quickly as possible.
- Make sure players are setting their feet properly before throwing to the next base.
- Stress making good throws to the receiver's chest and using two hands to receive the ball.

Variations

- Count the number of successful throws in a row and try to break the record each time.
- If more than one player is at each base, players can circle around and stay at the same base, or they can run to the next base after they throw.

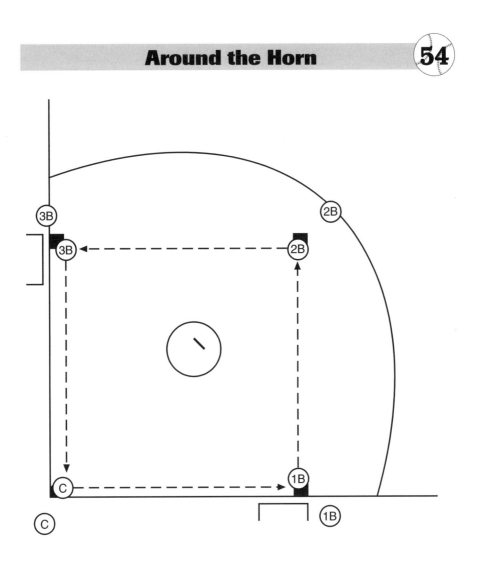

Scoop and Shoot

Purpose: To improve a quick release and shoestring catches. This drill contains a heavy conditioning element.

Procedure

1. Start with one or more players at each base. Begin with the ball at home plate.

2. A player from third base runs toward home. The player at home has a ball and throws a short-hop toss to the player running from third. That player catches the toss and tosses the ball back to the player at home. The player who fielded the ball goes to the end of the line at home. The player at home does a quick-feet turn and throws the ball to the next base (first). She then runs toward first. The player at first tosses a short hop to the player running from home. The fielder fields it and tosses it back to the player at first and goes to the end of that line. The player at first does a quick-feet turn and throws to second base and so on around the bases.

3. Continue running and tossing around the bases for as long as desired. Count the number of successful throws, and try to beat the record each time.

Key Points

- The toss should be below the receiver's knees; tossers can also throw one-hoppers.
- The tosser should receive the ball from the fielder with two hands and throw it to the next base as quickly as possible to practice quick feet.

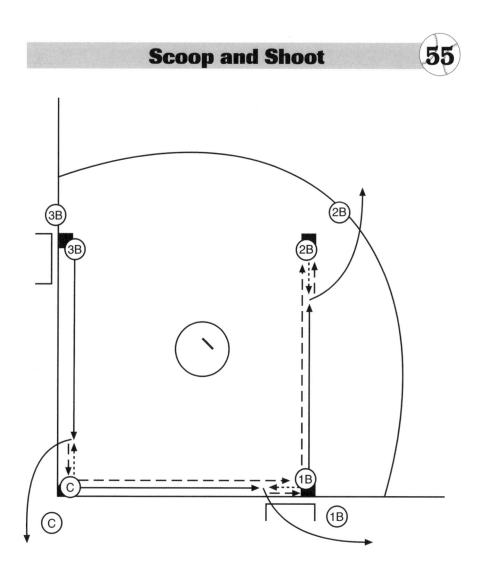

Three-Player Fungo

Purpose: To maximize the number of ground balls and fly balls being fielded in the least amount of time and thus improve overall fielding, to improve eye-hand coordination (through fungoing the ball), and to maximize the number of players involved.

Procedure

1. Start with one player ready to field ground balls or fly balls from a fungo hitter. Depending on the fielder's defensive position, the player and fungo hitter move closer or farther apart. Infielders should be on the infield at the proper position depth, and outfielders should be in the outfield or at outfield depth if inside. A third player stands next to the fungoer to receive throws from the fielder.

2. Hit 10 balls at the fielder and then rotate. The fungo hitter becomes the fielder, the receiver becomes the hitter, and the fielder becomes the receiver.

3. Perform for 10-15 minutes.

Key Points

- Make sure the receiver stands so she is facing the player hitting ground balls, not standing behind her.
- The whole team can do this drill at the same time, across the infield and outfield.

Variation

- Dump a bucket of balls by the fungoer, then put it out by the fielder so she can toss the balls into it instead of throwing them back.

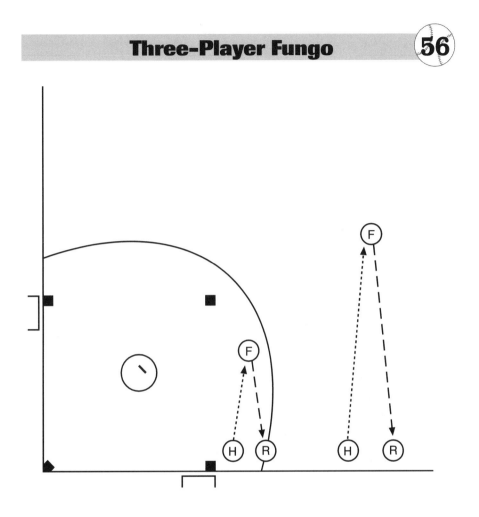

Line Fielding

Purpose: To warm up the infielders and outfielders and allow for repetition, therefore improving basic fielding skills on grounders and fly balls.

Procedure

1. Establish three to four lines of fielders: a corners line, a middle infielders line, and an outfielders line (if pitchers are included, they can form a separate line or join the corners). The coaches or players hitting the balls are on a foul line, facing the infield.

2. The fielders set up at the start of the line at their appropriate position depths.

3. The hitters hit each player two grounders or fly balls. The fielder then rotates to the back of the line after fielding two balls. Players can throw the balls back or place them in a bucket.

4. Perform for 10-15 minutes.

Key Points

- This drill can be done every day as a team warm-up.
- Pitchers should also participate at a corner depth. They can do a windup just prior to the ball being hit.

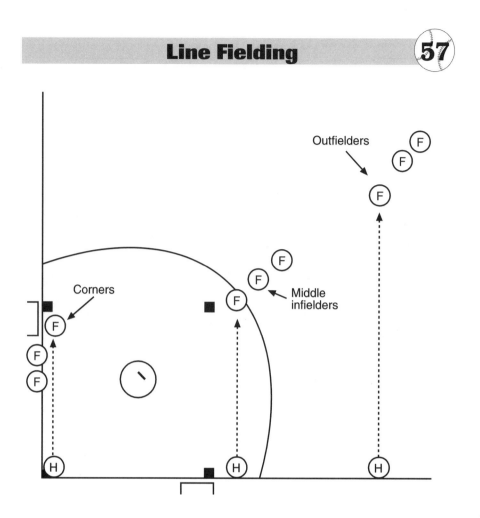

Figure 8

Purpose: To improve quickness and glove handling. The Figure 8 provides a good conditioning element as well.

Procedure

1. A fielder stands between two cones that are approximately 20 feet apart. A tosser sets up with 10 balls approximately 20 feet from the fielder but directly in front of her.

2. The fielder begins by running toward a cone while the tosser throws a soft line drive toward the cone. The fielder runs and reaches to catch it. Once it is caught the fielder throws the ball out of the way and heads toward the other cone. The tosser then throws a soft line drive toward that cone. The fielder again catches it and gets rid of it quickly.

3. The fielder continues running around the cones and switching directions in a figure 8 pattern.

4. Each player catches two sets of 10 balls.

Key Points

- Make sure the fielder turns the glove into appropriate positions. When moving to the glove hand (forehand) side, the glove pocket must face the tosser, or infield in game situations, at all times with the palm pointing up. When moving to the throwing hand side (backhand), the glove pocket must still face the tosser, but the fingers will be facing straight down.

- The fielder must quickly get rid of the ball and continue running the entire time.

- Have the tosser mix in medium-hard throws with soft line drives.

Figure 8

58

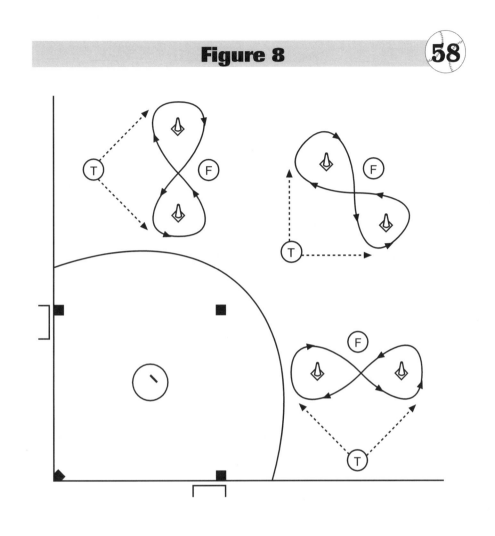

Box Grounders

Purpose: To get repetitions of ground balls and help preserve the player's throwing arm.

Procedure

1. Four players are used in each group. The players pair up and form a rectangle; position the players depending on the depth usually played by their position (i.e., middle depth, corner depth, outfield depth).

2. One player from each pair has a bat and their partners each have a glove and are set up in the ready position. Make sure the fielders are positioned to the front side of the hitters, diagonal from each other.

3. The two hitters hit each fielder a ground ball at the same time. After the balls are fielded, the fielders toss the balls to the hitting partners directly beside them.

4. Repeat this for 10-20 ground balls and then switch hitters and fielders.

Key Points

- Emphasize fielding the ball first with proper technique.
- More than one group can perform this drill at the same time.

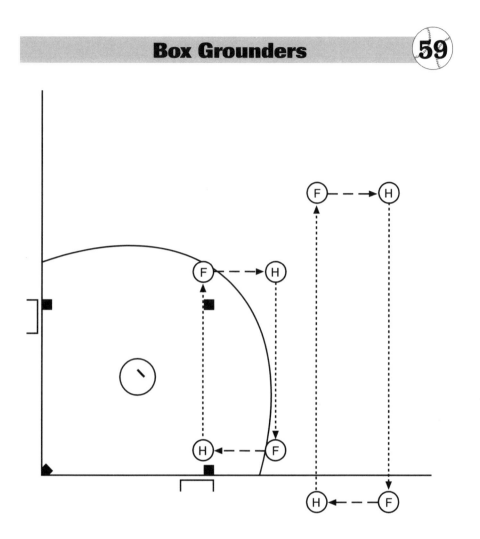

Range Fielding

Purpose: To practice diving, backhands, and forehands, and to demonstrate the range added when a player dives. This drill contains a strong conditioning element as well.

Procedure

1. Split the team into two groups; have half begin at third base and the other half at first base. The group at first faces home, and the group at third faces second. One person hitting ground balls is at second base and another is at home.

2. The player at first base begins running toward second, watching for the ball being hit from home. The fungoer at home hits a ground ball toward second base, ahead of the fielder. At the same time, the fielder at third base runs toward home and the fungoer at second hits a ground ball toward home plate.

3. If the fielders cannot reach the balls by staying on their feet they must dive no matter where the ball is.

4. After fielding the balls the fielders can toss them to the players hitting the ground balls and continue running, on to the other line.

5. Each player fields/dives 10-15 times then switches directions.

Key Points

- Players must dive even if they think the ball is out of range.

- Once the backhand dive is covered, switch the direction in which the fielders run. The group at first base runs toward home and the group at third base runs toward second base so they will have forehand dives (for right-handers). The hitter at home hits out toward the middle and shortstop area, and the hitter at second hits toward home plate.

Variation

- Fungoers can hit close pop-ups either in front of or behind the fielders.

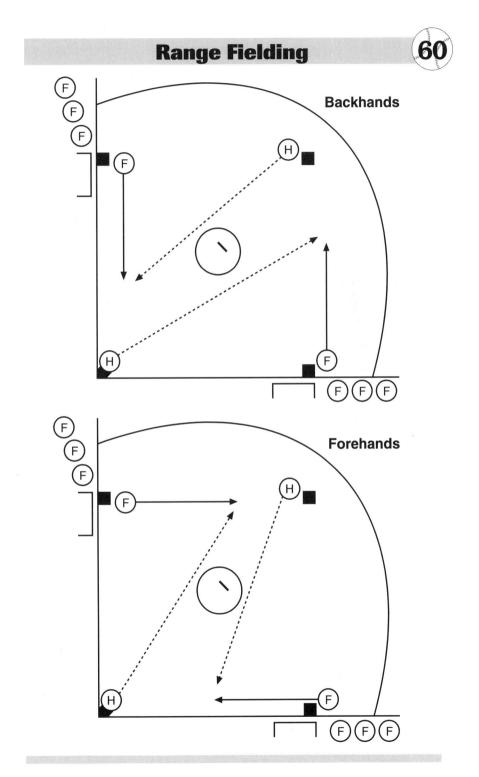

Backhands

Forehands

61   Hit the Cutoff

Purpose: To teach outfielders to hit the cutoff or relay person for all balls hit past them and to give the middle infielders practice serving as the relay person.

Procedure

1. Begin with at least one outfielder in right, center, and left fields. Spread three balls out behind each fielder close to the fence line. A shortstop and second baseman are needed in the infield.

2. Starting with the right fielder and taking turns, each outfielder starts in ready position at her normal depth.

3. The coach says, "Go," and the first fielder sprints to the ball, picks it up on her back foot, and throws to the relay person, who comes out to get the ball. The outfielder should be required to throw 60 percent of the distance between where the ball lies and home plate. If the ball is hit on the left side, the shortstop goes out and is the relay person while the second baseman covers second. If it is hit on the right side, the second baseman goes out and the shortstop covers second. If it is hit up the middle, the two middle infielders communicate and decide for themselves. (Ideally you'd like the player with the stronger arm to take as many relay throws as possible.)

4. When that play is complete the middle infielders reset, and the center fielder, then the left fielder, go back for a ball and make the same play.

5. Continue until each outfielder has thrown at least three balls.

Key Points

- Each outfielder should surround the ball before they get to it with the body already in position to throw.

- The outfielder should throw high, aiming for the relay person's head.

- The middle infielders may have to adjust how far they go out to get the ball depending on the strength of each outfielder's arm.

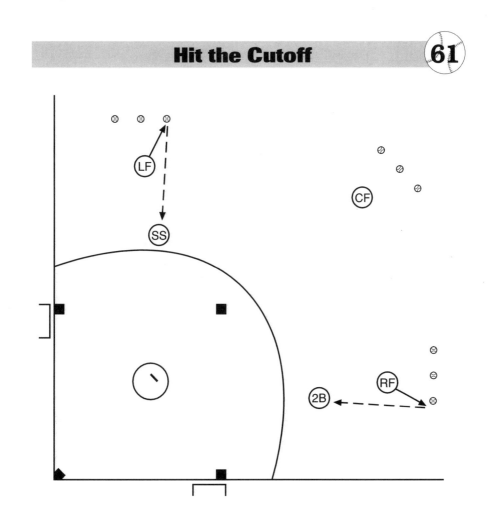

62 Relays and Cutoffs

Purpose: To establish a good system to relay the ball from an outfielder, primarily with runners on base.

Procedure

1. Start with the three outfielders in position. Place three balls behind each outfielder, near the fence. A catcher, two middle infielders, and a first baseman are also needed.

2. The left fielder begins by turning and running to get one ball, as in **drill #61, Hit the Cutoff**. The shortstop goes out to be the relay, placing herself so the outfielder throws 60 percent of the distance from the ball to home plate, and calls for the ball.

3. The catcher directs the shortstop to line up with home plate by yelling, "Left, left!" or "Right, right!" then "Hold!" At the same time, the first baseman lines herself up between the ball where it lies and home plate, positioning herself around the pitcher's mound area. The idea is to have the ball, the middle infielder, and the cutoff person all in a straight throwing line.

4. The outfielder surrounds the ball and picks it up on her back foot. She turns and throws toward the shortstop, aiming for her head. The shortstop moves to catch the ball on her glove side, opening up (drop steps back) as the ball approaches. If the ball is thrown short she should move out and catch it on the fly.

5. The shortstop then turns and throws to home, aiming at the first baseman's head. The first baseman moves to allow the ball to pass on her throwing side. If the catcher yells "Cut!" the first baseman cuts the ball. The catcher should also tell the first baseman what to do with the ball (e.g., "Cut hold," "Cut two"). If no cut is called, then the first baseman allows the ball to pass by her and arrive at home plate. The throw should be low and bounce once to the plate.

6. Each outfielder throws three balls.

Key Point

- The cutoff person must follow the ball as long as possible in case of a late cut call by the catcher. She should not cut the ball unless the catcher tells her to or if the throw is errant.

Variations

- The coach can designate the pitcher as the cutoff on the infield. If not, the pitcher should be backing up the play either at third base or home plate.
- Fungo balls over the heads of the outfielders instead of presetting the balls on the ground.

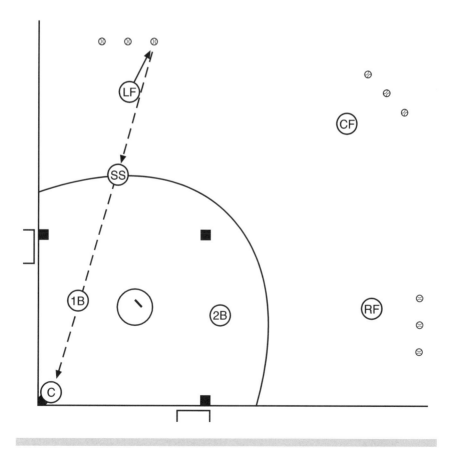

Fielding Batting Practice

Purpose: To get a defensive, gamelike workout in a routine batting practice. This drill also provides baserunning practice and conditioning for runners.

Procedure

1. Place a defensive team in the field and have a pitcher pitch to one or more hitters at the plate.
2. The defense plays out all hits as if it were a game. Set runners on bases as desired, and have base runners run as if in an actual game, practicing their baserunning at the same time.
3. Continue until all of the hitters have batted, switching with the fielders if desired.

Key Points

- Watch for lapses in intensity in the fielders, since down time with no hits can be long for some of the players.
- Completely play out each hit.

Variations

- For a shorter drill, the coach can start each at bat with a pitch count, such as two balls and one strike.
- The coach can pitch to the hitters instead.

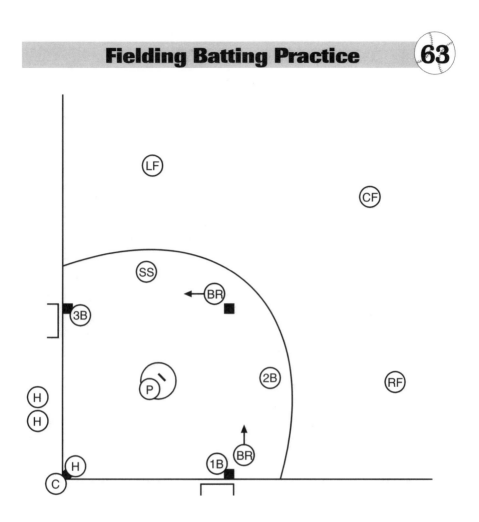

64. Infielders Run for Outfielders

Purpose: To practice live, gamelike situations with the outfielders. This drill also provides baserunning practice and conditioning for runners.

Procedure

1. Begin with outfielders in their defensive positions. Use all outfielders on the team for this drill, letting them take turns one at a time at each position. Also place a defensive player at first base, in the catcher's box, and at both middle infield positions. The other infielders will serve as base runners.
2. The coach places runners at desired bases and fungos from home plate.
3. Fungo grounders and/or fly balls to outfielders and have them execute defensive plays as needed. Runners run as if they were on base or hitting the ball.
4. Fungo until each outfielder has made 8-10 plays.

Key Points

- Simulate all game situations, using single and multiple runners as necessary.
- Base runners should wear helmets.

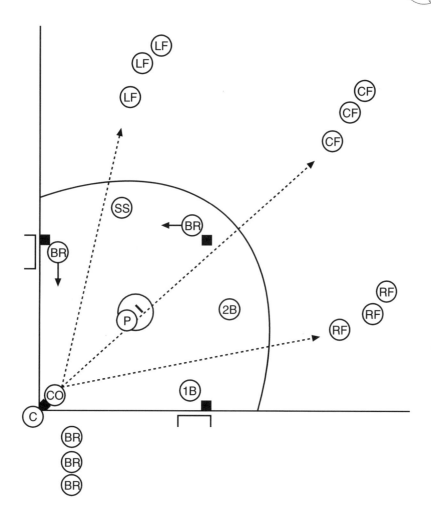

Outfielders Run for Infielders

Purpose: To practice live, gamelike situations with the infielders. This drill also provides baserunning practice and conditioning for runners.

Procedure

1. Begin with infielders in their defensive positions. Use all infielders on the team for this drill, letting them take turns one at a time at each position. The outfielders will serve as base runners.
2. The coach places runners at desired bases and fungos from home plate.
3. Fungo grounders and/or fly balls to infielders and have them execute defensive plays as needed. Runners run as if they were on base or hitting the ball.
4. Fungo until each infielder has made 8-10 plays.

Key Points

- Simulate all game situations, using single and multiple runners as necessary.
- Base runners should wear helmets.

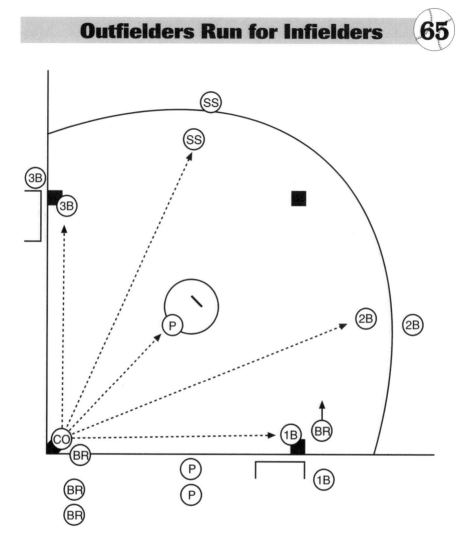

Purpose: To create gamelike defensive situations. This drill also provides baserunning practice and conditioning for runners.

Procedure

1. Place the defensive players, including the catcher, in their positions (a pitcher is optional). Extra players should run with helmets on.
2. Create defensive situations by placing runners at a certain base to begin the inning. The coach fungos from home plate, and the runners and defense play it out like they would in a game.
3. Play the innings out or just keep repeating a certain situation until it is mastered.
4. Perform for 20-30 minutes.

Key Point

- Controlled fungo should be the most gamelike practice next to a live scrimmage. Create any and all situations that might arise in an actual game.

Variations

- If a defensive player makes a mistake you feel was avoidable, rotate a new player in her position to create gamelike pressure. Use this variation when coaching advanced players at an advanced level of competition.
- Include pitchers in this drill.
- Perform this drill using only the infielders and eliminate balls hit to the outfield.

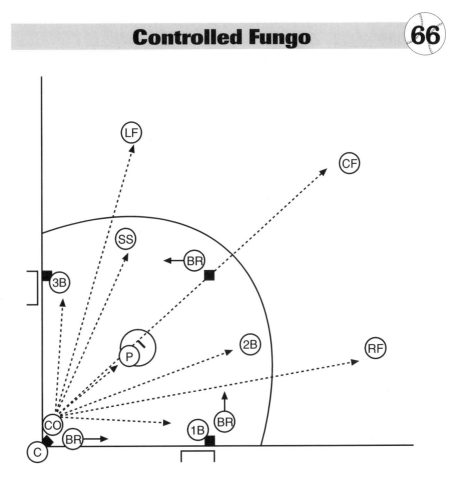

6
Practice Organization

Organizing effective practice sessions is one of the most important jobs of any successful coach. To help your players grow as athletes, you must teach them how to perform skills and drills correctly; maximizing quality repetitions in your practice sessions is a must. This chapter helps you determine which skills your players need to work on before the season begins. Sample practice plans are presented at the end of the chapter to show you how to conduct your practices effectively and efficiently, and special considerations for teaching youths to more advanced players are also discussed to help you maximize your practice sessions for all levels.

STARTING THE SEASON

Before you meet with your team for the first practice of the season, list the skills and plays that must be covered before opening day. Whether you practice indoors or outdoors, the basic skills are the same. A typical list might include the following skills:

Infielders

- Footwork at the bases—force outs, tag plays, and double plays
- Throwing to bases
- Checking the runner
- Fielding fundamentals
    - Grounders, including forehands and backhands
    - Pop-ups and communication
    - Diving
- First and third situations
- Fielding bunts

Pitchers

- Fielding bunts
- Throwing to bases
- Running the ball to first
- Covering home plate on a passed ball or wild pitch

- Intentional walks
- Pitchouts
- Backup responsibilities

Catchers

- Receiving balls and setting up
- Blocking pitches in the dirt
- Framing pitches
- Pop-ups
- Plays at the plate
  - Force outs
  - Tag plays (blocking the plate with a runner attempting to score)
- Fielding bunts
- Calling the game
- Cutoffs
- Throwing to bases
- Pitchouts
- Intentional walks
- Passed balls

Outfielders

- Grounders
  - Down and block
  - Like an infielder
  - On the charge
- Fly balls
  - Sun balls
  - Drop step for balls over the head
  - Playing the fence
- Line drives
- Throwing to bases
- Backup responsibilities

Team Skills

- Throwing and catching fundamentals
- Communication on all plays
- Rundowns
- Relays and cutoffs
- Hitting
- Bunting
- Baserunning
- Pickoffs

Don't forget to consider your team's strength and conditioning needs when planning your practices. For example, you might plan to include time for your team to lift weights after practice on Mondays, Wednesdays, and Fridays and do an aerobic conditioning workout after practice on Tuesdays and Thursdays. Tailor your workouts to match your team's and the individual players' needs.

GENERAL GUIDELINES

Good coaches constantly develop and modify their practices based on their players' skill levels and needs. Some fundamental guidelines should be followed, however, when planning every practice, from your shortest pregame practices to your longest preseason workouts.

- **Planning**—Planning is the key to a successful practice. Plan each minute of practice, including the number of players needed, the specific players involved, the equipment needed, and the distribution of coaches in the groups (if you have the luxury of having assistants!) for each activity or drill. Planning each minute does not necessarily mean you have to stick to your original plan with no changes. Many times if I am not satisfied with the way a drill is going, we stay with it longer. And often times the opposite is true, and we end up moving on quicker than I had planned if the players have already mastered the skill in question. Solid planning in advance actually allows for greater flexibility. It also gives you a record and reference for future seasons.

- **Program goals**—You should have a mental picture in your mind of what you would like to accomplish in all areas of the program. Make your goals broad—"With the talent we have I think we can be state champs this year"—as well as detailed—"Let's get through team warm-ups without throwing any balls away." Goals and goal setting can be an entire book in itself. The important thing is to set goals for every aspect of your program. You have to have a vision of where you want to go before you can decide on how you are going to get there.

- **Skill levels**—Your entire program must be structured around the highest level of competition you will face during your season. It is not beneficial to the players to succeed easily every day in practice but then get beaten badly during games because they aren't ready for competition. Drills and practices need to be adjusted so that the players are challenged; you'll find many variations to the drills in this book to help you start modifying the drills to suit your needs.

Preparing your players for competition doesn't mean you should make every drill as difficult as you can for each player. Psychologically, players need to experience some level of success each practice session. I like to take the "sandwich approach" to practices. I start with a drill or skill that the players will be successful doing, then move to more challenging skills and practice in the middle of the session (the meat of practice), then finish the practice with another drill or technique that they can execute successfully. At no time, however, do I give the team credit or let them off the hook (by moving on to the next drill) for skills that are not executed correctly. I do not believe in giving the players a false sense of how good they are or how good we are as a team. I do not mean that coaches should be negative, but we should not give players inaccurate evaluations of their skills. Instead, honestly assess each player's abilities and the abilities of the team as a whole. With thoughtful feedback from their coach, your players will know what to work on to improve their skills.

- **Time**—Developing simple routines for warm-ups, hitting stations, and defensive drills can save a lot of time in the long run. Establishing team procedures involves teaching the players generally how we practice—the typical way in which we do things—from explaining, "This is how we warm up" to "This is how we behave in the dugout" and everything in between. Developing routines is an important part of saving time. Team procedures allow the players to become familiar with the general setup so that you don't have to waste a lot of time reexplaining drills or techniques at every practice. Designate one of your first days of practice as a "drill day." Teach the whole team how to set up for all of the drills you plan on using in your upcoming practices. In addition, teach all players how to fungo hit to help you delegate tasks and maximize your practice efficiency. This will allow you to make the most of your available practice time, whether it is 1 hour or 3 hours long. One of your goals for practice is to have all of the players doing something all of the time—no one should just be standing around. Whether it's performing a drill or serving as a tosser, hitter, or receiver in another drill, a player can always be doing something.

The number of practice sessions and the amount of time for practice also have an impact on what the coach can accomplish. High school coaches cannot necessarily expect to spend the amount of time on strength and conditioning as college-level coaches do. Prioritizing skills is even more important for those programs that are dealing with space and time limitations.

• **Equipment**—You'll need a very short equipment list to execute all of the drills in this book. I personally started my career with a very small equipment budget, and I still operate much the same way today. You may find the following basic equipment list helpful in using the drills in this book:

- Fungo bat—I use a lightweight bat that my team no longer uses in games.
- Several dozen balls (eight minimum)—We try to keep a dozen balls separate for throwing and a couple of good balls available for total team drills like controlled fungo.
- Ball buckets (four minimum)— I like to use old industrial paint buckets for holding the balls instead of using ball bags.
- Construction-type cones (four)—These cones can be any size, but if you can get the tall ones they can double as batting Ts.

- Catchers' equipment including masks.

- **Space**—The design of the practice will obviously depend on the space available. It is a good idea to draw a picture of the facility, and then lay out the practice within the picture. Decide on how the players will rotate through the facility. Drill stations are helpful for getting a big group through a small space in a short amount of time. Just be careful not to sacrifice quality of repetitions for quantity of repetitions.

- **Support staff**—If necessary it is possible to coach a team by yourself, but you will have to be that much more organized. Consider splitting the team into smaller groups as much as possible. For instance, each position group could come to practice at a different time or on different days. Later you can combine whole group drills once basic skills have been taught.

  Coaching a team is much easier for both the coach and players if you hire or solicit the help of one or more assistants. Defining assistants' roles clearly and giving them feedback often will make your job easier and more rewarding. Remember that your own players can be a great help. Show them how to help and encourage their teammates in practice. I teach all our players to fungo and front toss pitch from a short distance. That way any two players can take grounders or flys and do batting practice on their own if need be.

- **Creativity**—Although players may not expect the coach to be a recreation director, you don't want to lose your players' interest and enthusiasm to boredom. Change the workouts and practices periodically to keep your players' attention. I keep drill books and old practice plans handy so I can add a new drill when things get stale.

- **Intensity**—It's true that teams play how they practice! The key to developing a consistent defense is to practice with the same intensity with which you play the game. Once practice begins, players should be focused and working hard to execute each skill under gamelike conditions at all times. Execute the drills as close to game speed as possible, and have the same expectations for practice that you have in games. For example, a team that plays catch well during warm-ups is likely to have fewer throwing errors during games. It is reasonable, therefore, to expect to have no overthrows during warm-ups.

• **Mental training**—I strongly believe that any quality program must incorporate some mental training into the practice plan. Mental toughness is a critical component of any quality player and team. Mental training skills that are helpful include (but are not limited to) relaxation techniques, imagery, goal setting, developing a positive mental attitude, creating precompetition routines, and developing concentration and focus. Coaches should not be scared off by this growing field; getting players to overachieve is what coaching is all about.

Mental skills, however, can only do so much. The coach must recognize when players simply don't have the ability to execute certain skills. It's a tough tradeoff between devoting time to mental training versus training in the fundamentals of the game. I like to incorporate as much mental training directly into practice as I can. The great thing about mental skills is that they are skills the players will use to enhance every aspect of their lives long after their softball career is over. Some excellent resources are available for you to consult. If you would like specific recommendations, please call the National Fastpitch Coaches Association (573-875-3033) for assistance.

• **Strength and conditioning**—Quality programs must also address the team's strength and conditioning needs. Players over the age of 12 should be able to begin a lifting program. Prior to playing softball at the college level, players should be using a lifting program designed for total overall fitness. Players should have quality supervision when lifting until they have mastered the proper techniques. Maintaining flexibility should be incorporated as part of any lifting program.

Players should also maintain a general level of conditioning. I have found that many of the softball players I have worked with do not enjoy running. I try to overcome this obstacle by incorporating as many different types of conditioning workouts into practice as possible. For example, some days we do a lot of baserunning and on other days we incorporate a good mix of drills that include a conditioning element. We also condition outside of practice year round at a minimum of two days per week. Conditioning activities include swimming, biking, various types of running and track work, plyometrics, and aerobics.

SPECIAL CONSIDERATIONS FOR YOUTH TO ADVANCED LEVEL ATHLETES

As I emphasize throughout this chapter, planning is the key to successful practices. It is very important that you schedule your team's practices carefully while taking into consideration the variety of factors that affect your workouts, including the players' skill levels; the time, space, and equipment that are available; and the skills and techniques that need to be covered. This section begins with a discussion of some of the unique situations that coaches of each level from youth teams to more advanced athletes need to consider when planning practices for their teams, and ends with three intermediate to advanced sample practice plans for focusing on offense, defense, and a combination of the two.

Youth Teams

Kids play the game of softball for the simple reason that it is fun. Some girls, however, will play more seriously as they get older because they truly enjoy the challenge of the game. It is important when coaching younger athletes (ages 14 and under) to concentrate on the fundamentals of the game and on sportsmanship issues. Practices should last between 1-1/2 and 2 hours at most.

When coaching players at this level, schedule a day to meet with all the parents to discuss the dos and don'ts of the program. This is also a good time to solicit their help at practices and games—just be sure to clearly define their role and yours on the team. Everything should be taught from a positive standpoint. The Women's Sports Foundation (800-227-3988) and local clinics can be excellent resources for the youth coach.

Intermediate Teams

Intermediate teams (ages 14-16) have many of the same limitations as do youth teams. Not all players are motivated to play for the same reasons. Some players in this group are now serious players, but many are still in the game for social reasons. I believe that kids tend to gravitate toward the sports and skills that they do best. You should certainly expect more from them athletically, and the levels and length of concentration should be better (practices can usually last between 2 and 2-1/2 hours). Continue to concentrate on the basic fundamentals of the game while beginning to address more seriously the defensive and offensive situations the team will encounter in their games with other teams.

Advanced Teams

I consider advanced teams to be any team that will compete in the top 20 of any high school division and any summer club team in the 16 and under division all the way up to the NCAA division I. You can and should expect players on these teams to be able to maintain a game-level intensity throughout your practice session. Teams at this level tend to have one or more assistant coaches, and practices become more complex by covering multiple skills in one day. I do not recommend constant practice for longer than 2 to 2-1/2 hours; however, if you are going two days or longer between practices, the sessions can run longer. At Michigan State we practice five to six days a week for 2 to 2-1/2 hours each session (not counting separate strength and conditioning and pitching workouts). I have specific goals in mind for each practice, and if we accomplish those goals in a shorter amount of time it's acceptable to end a little early.

Sample Practice Plans

The following sample plans are geared for intermediate to advanced level teams, but can be scaled back for younger teams. When planning each practice, consider having certain positions (pitchers and catchers, middles) come earlier than the rest of the team to focus on certain skills. Organize each practice in detail; when dividing the team by positions or working on small group or partner drills, plan ahead which players will be partners in both defensive and offensive drills so practice will run smoothly with no confusion.

SAMPLE PRACTICE PLAN 1
FOCUS ON OFFENSE

2:30 p.m.	Pitchers and catchers come early for individual work.
3:00 p.m.	Middles practice fielding, various plays
3:30 p.m.	Entire team: Jogging, stretching, and warm-up throws
3:50 p.m.	Defensive/offensive split practice Pitchers (outfielders receive throws) • **Five-Ball Drill, #10** • **Throwing to Bases, #23** • **Run the Ball to First, #24** Outfielders (pitchers receive throws at bases) • Focus on all fielding—grounders, flys, and line drives Infielders and catchers • Hitting drills
4:20 p.m.	Defensive/offensive split practice (switch) Infielders (catchers practice at their other position, fungo, or receive balls) • Situations with runner at second • Situations with runner at third • **Controlled Fungo, #66** Pitchers and outfielders • Hitting drills
4:50 p.m.	**Fielding Batting Practice, #63** • Runner at second with no outs (play out inning)

(continued)

SAMPLE PRACTICE PLAN 1
FOCUS ON OFFENSE *(continued)*

	• Runner at third with no outs (play out inning)
5:15 p.m.	Weightlifting
5:45 p.m.	Announcements, end practice

SAMPLE PRACTICE PLAN 2
FOCUS ON DEFENSE

2:30 p.m.	Pitchers and catchers come early for individual work.
3:00 p.m.	Open hitting practice
3:30 p.m.	Entire team: Jogging, stretching, and warm-up throws
3:50 p.m.	**Diamond Drill, #51**
4:00 p.m.	**Line Fielding, #57**
4:15 p.m.	**Multiple Infield, #14** (Two hitters hit 7-10 balls each per round, with no runners.) **Round 1** *Ball 1* • Hitter 1—Second baseman fields and throws to shortstop covering second base, and vice versa. • Hitter 2—Third baseman fields and throws to first base.

SAMPLE PRACTICE PLAN 2
FOCUS ON DEFENSE

Ball 2

- Hitter 1—Left fielder fields and throws to second.
- Hitter 2—Center fielder fields and throws to third.

Round 2

Ball 1

- Hitter 1—Third baseman and first baseman field and throw to first (backup first baseman covers first).
- Hitter 2—Shortstop and second baseman field and throw to third (backup third baseman covers third).

Ball 2

- Hitter 1—Left fielder fields and throws home.
- Hitter 2—Center fielder fields and throws to second.

Round 3

Ball 1

- Hitter 1—Third baseman fields ball and touches third for force out.
- Hitter 2—Second baseman and short-stop field and throw to first.

Ball 2

- Hitter 1—Center fielder fields and throws home.
- Hitter 2—Right fielder fields and throws to first on line drive grounders.

5:00 p.m.	Baserunning practice
5:30 p.m.	Announcements, end practice

SAMPLE PRACTICE PLAN 3
FOCUS ON OFFENSE AND DEFENSE

2:30 p.m. Pitchers and catchers come early for individual work.

3:30 p.m. Entire team: Jogging, stretching, and warm-up throws

3:50 p.m. **Quarterback Catch, #52** (2 lines)

3:55 p.m. **Line Fielding, #57**

4:10 p.m. Defensive/offensive split practice
Pitchers
- **Fielding Bunts, #21**
- **Fielding Squeeze Bunts, #22**
- **Throwing to Bases, #23**
- **Plate Coverage on a Wild Pitch, #25**

Outfielders
- Down and block, like an infielder, and on the charge techniques from chapter 1
- **Fly Balls—Partner Toss, #36** and **Sliding to the Foul Line Fence, #40**
- **Line Drives, #47**

Infielders and catchers
- Hitting drills

4:35 p.m. Defensive/offensive split practice (switch)
Infielders
(catchers practice at their other position, fungo, or receive balls)
Corners
- **Fielding Bunts, #7**

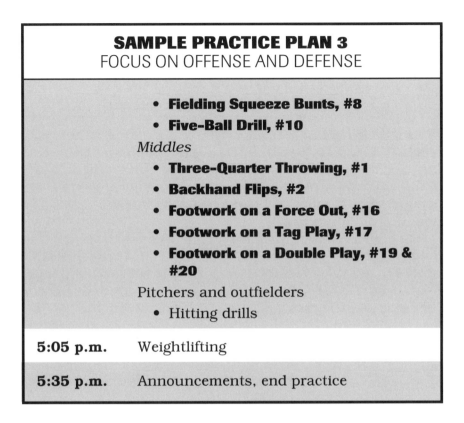

SAMPLE PRACTICE PLAN 3
FOCUS ON OFFENSE AND DEFENSE

- **Fielding Squeeze Bunts, #8**
- **Five-Ball Drill, #10**

Middles
- **Three-Quarter Throwing, #1**
- **Backhand Flips, #2**
- **Footwork on a Force Out, #16**
- **Footwork on a Tag Play, #17**
- **Footwork on a Double Play, #19 & #20**

Pitchers and outfielders
- Hitting drills

5:05 p.m.   Weightlifting

5:35 p.m.   Announcements, end practice

A WINNING DEFENSE

Good coaches in any sport possess similar traits. They

- have the ability to make people believe in themselves;
- are able to bring people together as a team to work toward a common goal;
- possess high expectations and are demanding of team performance;
- are encouraging and supportive;
- maintain discipline and give constructive feedback;
- are persistent—they never give up, they believe in hard work, and they learn from their mistakes;
- have a vision of competitive greatness;

- are enthusiastic;
- are driven by their own desire for personal excellence and are *technically competent;* and
- practice their own values.

This book addresses technical competence by giving you drills to help eliminate the opponent's big inning, to help play catch well, and work on the mental game to ensure a successful defense. In addition to the skills outlined in this book, other skills you will need to achieve technical competence are communication skills, problem-solving skills, counseling skills, and motivational skills.

Remember, players play the game because they have fun doing it. It is our job as coaches to teach them the skills necessary for them to be successful. We must give them these skills in such a way that even years after they are done playing they still love the game.

About the Author

Jacquie Joseph has seen much success in her young NCAA Division I head coaching career, which has spanned 10 years. She's coached at Michigan State University (MSU) since 1993 and she is also a USA Softball National Team coach, having participated at the USA Festival and for the Pan American qualifying team.

While at MSU, Joseph has led the Spartans to their best record and best Big Ten finish in school history. Prior to her MSU career, she coached Bowling Green University to a Mid-American Conference championship in 1993.

Joseph was elected President of the National Fastpitch Coaches Association in 1994, and is currently serving in her fourth year. This association represents all fastpitch coaches at the NCAA Division I, II, and III, junior college, NAIA, high school, and summer league levels.

When she's not coaching softball or on the road, Joseph enjoys playing golf and reading.